FROM TRAMS TO ARRIV
COLCHESTER, ESSE

1904 - 2004

by

R NICOLAS COLLINS

&

GEOFF R MILLS

An illustrated history of a century of passenger transport services provided by
Colchester Corporation Tramways in 1904 and the successors through to
Arriva Colchester Ltd in 2004.

Ex Libris

Michael I. Brown

ISBN 0 9527770 6 1

Published by: MW Transport Publications,
12 Saxon Close,
Lexden,
Colchester, Essex
CO3 4LH
Tel 01206 766886

Front Cover Pictures:
Top: Tram 10 is seen climbing from Lexden Road towards the Lexden terminus in London Road.
From a painting by Malcolm Root
Bottom: Bus 49 (H49MJN) is seen as Arriva 5409. One of three Leyland Olympians delivered to Colchester
Borough Transport in 1991, this was numerically the last new double-decker supplied to the municipal
operator and is seen in Colchester Bus Station during December 2002 on a schooldays only operation to
Coggeshall, a positioning journey to Honywood School.
GR Mills

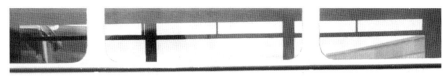

CHANGING
FLEET NAMES

Vehicle:
1949 Daimler CVD6/Roberts preserved in Lincoln. The only known half cab Colchester Corporation bus fully restored as original. Originally shaded gold leaf lettering on Tuscan red panels.

Fleet Name:
From May 1928 to April 1974 i.e. post trams to the reorganisation of local government.

Vehicle:
One of the thirty 1976-1980 Leyland AN68/ECW

Fleet Name:
Applied after April 1974 Red lettering on a cream painted body panel. Last bus so adorned left the town in January 2002.

Vehicle:
One of 1988-1991 Leyland Olympian/ECW

Fleet Name:
Applied after October 1997 White lettering above gold on aquamarine painted body panel. The words 'serving Colchester' were discontinued on all post 2003 repaints.

INTRODUCTION

This history of Colchester Corporation Transport and successors is a result of a lifetime's interest in buses by a pair of Colcestrians who met as school boys both observing the local transport scene. With the help of the then General Manager the late John Gray a full list of all the pre-war stock which had gone was established. Further research through every issue of the Essex County Standard from 1903 to the then present time was laboriously searched for any mention or reference to the borough transport to gain a complete picture of the past operations.

Nicolas Collins was educated at Endsleigh School in Lexden Road close to where he lived. After attaining qualifications he joined Colchester Corporation Transport as traffic clerk in 1960. After 14 years he left and joined the transportation co-ordination section of Essex County Council, returning to CBT in 1976 as traffic superintendent. He became Operations Director for the new company in October 1986 and took early retirement in October 1993 before the sale to the British Bus Group.

Geoff Mills' primary education was at St James Church of England school off East Hill, before passing the scholarship to attend the North East Essex Technical School on North Hill. After leaving school he initially served a 5 year apprenticeship as a structural detail draughtsman and gained an ONC (Building) certificate. Through his profession he befriended a bus/haulage operator and was able to prepare all the drawings and clerk of works the creation of a new operating centre with workshops and a large covered parking area. In return he was trained and passed an all groups PSV test. This enabled part-time work to be undertaken for any of a wide variety of operators and he can claim to have driven for every independent stage carriage provider serving Colchester over the past 35 years. For the past five years he has worked part-time for Arriva and thus achieved a lifetime's ambition to drive buses from Magdalen Street Depot the original source of a half a century of research.

CONTENTS

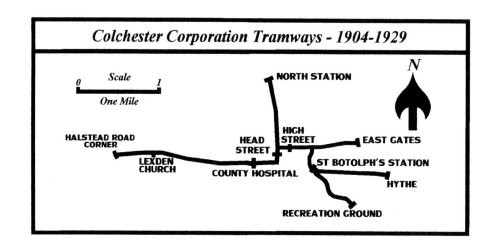

Colchester Corporation Tramways - 1904-1929

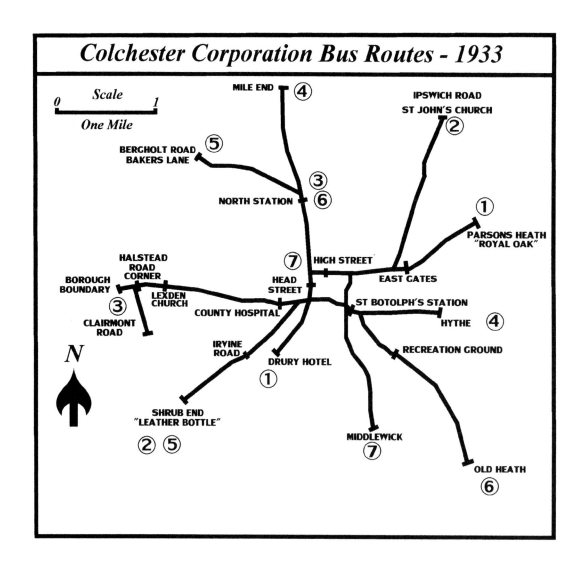

Colchester Corporation Bus Routes - 1933

COLCHESTER 1904 - 2004

Municipal Public Transport in Colchester began in 1904 after Colchester Corporation had sought powers in 1900 to operate a system of electric tramways in the Borough but it took four years before the system became operational. There had been two previous attempts to provide trams in the town, the first in 1883 by Arthur George Fenn and Frank Whitmore to operate steam trams, and in 1899 the British Electric Traction Co sought powers which were refused in favour of the municipal operation.

In January 1904 the rails for the 3ft 6in gauge track were delivered by ship from Belgium to the Hythe on the River Colne and were then hauled on trolleys pulled by traction engines to the routes. Various difficulties were encountered during the construction of the tramway: The 60ft length of the rails caused problems when the traction engines damaged pavements and some water mains were cracked; a tower wagon overturned at Lexden when workmen were erecting a post for the overhead lines; it was necessary to widen the bridge over the Colne at Middleborough and to lower the road under the railway bridge at North Station.

The system consisted of a mixture of double track and single track with loops. One interesting feature was a signalling system for the single track at the corner of Queen Street with High Street and also at Headgate.

The trams were delivered to the depot in Magdalen Street in July 1904. There were 16 trams supplied by Dick Kerr & Co which had two 35hp motors and Brill 21E trucks. The bodies were built by the Electric Railway and Tramway Carriage Works Ltd of Preston and seated 22 passengers inside and 24 outside on wooden slatted seats. The trams cost £575 each and were of an unusual design in that they had reversed staircases and trolleypoles set to one side. As the starting date approached frequent tests were made and, on the evening when town councillors took a ride to Lexden, the current failed and the tram (no 13) came to an abrupt halt.

The Tramway Opens

The system was opened to the public on 28 July 1904 in pouring rain with a ceremony performed by the Mayoress on tram 13, this was followed by a run to Lexden and return to North Station before arriving back at the Town Hall. A 15 minute frequency service was provided on three cross town routes:

    North Station and Lexden
    North Station and East Gates
    North Station and Hythe

These gave a combined frequency of every 5 minutes between North Station and the top of High Street/North Hill junction. The first trams started at 5.00 a.m. on Mondays to Saturdays and 9.00 a.m. on Sundays and the services ran until 11.30 p.m., but over the next two years early and late services, and the Sunday timetables, were reduced.

The only extension to the system was that from St Botolphs along the Military Road to the Old Heath Recreation Ground which opened in July 1906. Two more trams were purchased which differed from the others in that they had normal facing staircases. The trams had a relatively uneventful life and no further extensions took place. Towards the end, however, the track was in a poor condition and there were several derailments.

Tragedy

Mention should be made of an event that took place on Saturday 12 July 1913. A horrific railway accident had occurred just west of Colchester North Station when the Cromer Express collided with a light locomotive and three railwaymen died. Considerable disruption followed and some trains from London stopped at Chitts Hill level crossing where passengers alighted and walked to Lexden to be conveyed on a special service of trams which had been laid on. The tram service continued throughout the night with all available staff remaining on duty - a very early example of a railway replacement service! Ironically a tram derailed at the bottom of Lexden Hill the next day but there were no serious casualties.

The Colchester Corporation Act 1927 provided for tramway replacement with provision for motor bus operation anywhere in the Borough and trolleybuses on the tram routes, the latter never being taken up. The presentation of the Bill to Parliament brought an offer from the National Omnibus Co to operate bus services in the Borough with a yearly payment to the Council of £550. Similar offers were received from local operators S Blackwell & Sons of Earls Colne, A W Berry & Sons of Colchester and Mr. A Warburton of Headingley, Leeds. None of these offers was accepted and with the passing of the Act tramway replacement commenced in 1928.

The first route to be withdrawn was that to East Gates which had already been curtailed at East Bridge while widening took place. On 21 March 1928, two new half hourly bus routes started, operating between Parsons Heath and Shrub End (Leather Bottle); and Greenstead Road (Hythe Station Road) and Butt Road (Drury Hotel). Four Dennis G's with Strachan & Brown 20 seat bodies were purchased for these services and were quickly followed by five Dennis E's and two double deck Dennis H's. From 1 October buses replaced the trams between Lexden and North Station.

TIMETABLE Pages from booklet

WEEK DAYS.

To North Station.
From Lexden.

Lexden depart.	Top High St. depart.	N'th Stn. arrive.
	7 23 a.m.	7 30 a.m.
	7 44	7 51
7 50 a.m.	8 5	8 12
	8 20	8 27
8 20	8 35	8 42
8 35	8 50	8 57
8 50	9 5	9 12
9 5	9 20	9 27

These times are repeated each hour of day, making a 15 minutes service to last cars, which run as follows:—

9 35 p.m.	9 50 p.m.	9 57 p.m.
9 50	10 5	To depôt.
10 5	10 20	To depôt.

5 mins. service from top of North Hill to North Station to 8 p.m., then 7½ mins. service to last cars.

9

WEEK DAYS.

To North Station.
From Hythe.

Hythe depart.	Top High St. depart.	N'th Stn. arrive.
7 46 a.m.	8 0 a.m.	8 7 am.
8 1	8 15	8 22
8 16	8 30	8 37
8 31	8 45	8 52
8 45	8 59	9 6

And every 15 minutes to—

7 31 p.m.	7 45 p.m.	7 52 p.m.
7 46	8 0	To depôt.
8 1	8 15 arrive.	
8 20	8 34	,,

And every 15 minutes to last cars, which run as follows:—

9 35 p.m.	9 49 p.m. arrive.	
9 49	To depôt.	
10 4	To depôt.	

5 mins. service from top of North Hill to North Station to 8 p.m., then 7½ mins. service to last cars.

10

WEEK DAYS.

To North Station.
From Recreation Grnd.

Recreation Ground depart.	Top of High Street depart.	North Station arrive.
7 42 a.m.	7 55 a.m.	8 2 a.m.
7 57	8 10	8 17
8 12	8 25	8 32
8 27	8 40	8 47

And every 15 minutes to—

7 59 p.m.	8 12 p.m.	8 19 p.m.

And every 15 minutes to last cars, which run as follows:—

9 29 p.m.	9 42 p.m.	9 49 p.m.
9 41	To depôt.	
9 56	To depôt.	

5 mins. service from top of North Hill to North Station to 8 p.m., then 7½ mins. service to last cars.

11

WEEK DAYS.

To North Station.
From East Gates.

East Gates depart.	High Street arrive.
7 54 a.m.	8 2 a.m.
8 20	8 29
8 40	8 49
9 0	9 9

These times are repeated each hour of day, making a 20 minutes service until—

12 58 p.m.	1 5 p.m.
1 14	1 22
1 31	1 39
1 50	1 59
2 20	2 29
2 40	2 49

And every 20 minutes to last car—

9 20 p.m.	9 29 p.m.
9 40	To depôt.

Passengers booking through to the North Station route change cars at the top of North Hill.

5 mins. service from top of North Hill to North Station to 8 p.m., then 7½ mins. service to last cars.

12

WEEK DAYS.

From North Station.
To Lexden.

N'th. Stn. depart.	Top High St. depart.	Lexden arrive.
	7 35 a.m.	7 50 a.m.
7 36 a.m.	7 43	
7 53	8 5	8 20
8 14	8 20	8 35
8 29	8 35	8 50
8 44	8 50	9 5
8 59	9 5	9 20

And every 15 minutes to—

9 44 p.m.	9 50 p.m.	10 5 p.m.
9 59	10 5	To depôt.

5 mins. service from North Station to top of North Hill to 8 p.m., then 7½ mins. service to last cars.

13

WEEK DAYS.

From North Station.
To Hythe.

North Station depart.	Top of High Street depart.	Hythe arrive.
8 10 a.m.	8 17 a.m.	8 31 a.m.
8 25	8 32	8 45
8 40	8 47	9 1
8 55	9 2	9 16

And every 15 minutes to—

7 55 p.m.	8 2 p.m.	8 16 p.m.
	8 20	8 34

And every 15 minutes to last car—

	9 50 p.m.	10 4 p.m.

5 mins. service from North Station to top of North Hill to 8 p.m.; then 7½ mins. service to last cars.

14

WEEK DAYS.

From North Station.
To Recreation Ground.

North Station depart.	Top of High Street depart.	Recreation Ground arrive.
8 5 a.m.	8 12 a.m.	8 25 a.m.
8 20	8 27	8 40
8 35	8 42	8 55
8 50	8 57	9 10

And every 15 minutes to—

8 5 p.m.	8 12 p.m.	8 25 p.m.
8 21	8 28	8 41

And every 15 minutes to last cars, which run as follows:—

8 51 p.m.	8 58 p.m.	9 11 p.m.
9 6	9 13	9 26
9 21	9 28	9 41
9 36	9 43	9 56
9 56	10 2	To depôt.

5 mins. service from North Station to top of North Hill to 8 p.m.; then 7½ mins. service to last cars.

15

WEEK DAYS.

From North Station.
To East Gates.

Top of High Street depart.	East Gates arrive.
8 5 a.m.	8 15 a.m.
8 30	8 39
8 50	8 59
9 10	9 19

These times are repeated each hour of day, making a 20 minutes service until—

12 50 p.m.	12 58 p.m.
1 5	1 13
1 22	1 30
1 40	1 49
2 0	2 10
2 30	2 39
2 50	2 59

And every 20 minutes to last car—

9 30 p.m.	9 39 p.m.

Passengers booking through from the North Station route to the East Gates route change cars at the top of North Hill.

5 mins. service from North Station to top of North Hill to 8 p.m.; then 7½ mins. service to last cars.

16

SUNDAYS.

To North Station.

From Lexden.

Lexden depart.	Top High St. depart.	North Stn. arrive.
9 25 a.m.	9 40 a.m.	9 47 a.m.
	9 55	10 2
10 10	10 25	10 32
10 33	10 48	To depôt.
12 35 p.m.	12 50 p.m.	12 57 p.m.
1 1	1 20	1 27
1 33	1 50	1 57
2 3	2 20	2 27
2 33	2 50	2 57
2 50	3 5	3 12
3 5	3 20	3 27
3 20	3 35	3 42
3 35	3 50	3 57

These times are repeated each hour of day, making a 15 minutes service to last cars, which run as follows :—

9 35 p.m.	9 50 p.m.	9 57 p.m.
9 50	10 5	To depôt.
10 5	10 20	To depôt.

5 mins. service from top of North Hill to North Station from 5 p.m.

17

SUNDAYS.

To North Station.

From Hythe.

Hythe depart.	Top of High Street depart.	North Station arrive.
	9 45 a.m.	9 52 a.m.
	10 5	10 12
10 0 a.m.	10 15	10 22
10 40	10 54	To depôt.
10 46	To depôt.	
12 25 p.m.	12 39 p.m.	
12 55	1 9	
1 25	1 39	
1 55	2 9	
2 25	2 38	
2 50	3 4	
3 5	3 19	
And every 15 minutes to		
4 35	4 48	
4 47	5 0	5 7 p.m.
5 1	5 15	5 22
And every 15 minutes to		
9 31 p.m.	9 45 p.m.	9 52
9 46	To depôt.	
10 1	To depôt.	

5 mins. service from top of North Hill to North Station from 5 p.m.

18

SUNDAYS.

To North Station.

From Recreation Gr'nd.

Recreation Ground depart.	Top of High Street depart.	North Station arrive.
9 37 am.	9 50 a.m.	9 57 a.m.
	10 10	10 17
10 40	10 52	To depôt.
	12 30 p.m.	12 40 p.m.
1 5 p.m.	1 16	
1 26	1 35	1 40
1 56	2 5	2 11
2 26	2 35	2 40
	2 57	3 4
2 59	3 12	3 19
3 14	3 27	3 34
And every 15 minutes to—		
4 44	4 57	5 4
4 57	5 10	5 17
And every 15 minutes to—		
9 27	9 40	9 47
9 40	To depôt.	
9 55	To depôt.	

5 mins. service from top of North Hill to North Station from 5 p.m.

19

SUNDAYS.

To North Station.

From East Gates.

East Gates depart.	Top of High Street depart.	North Station arrive.
9 50 a.m.	10 0 am.	10 7 a.m.
	10 20	10 27
10 45	10 54	To depôt.
12 40 p.m.	12 49 p.m.	
1 0	1 9	
1 20	1 29	

These times are repeated each hour of day, making a 20 minutes service to last cars, which run as follows :—

9 20	9 29
9 40	To depôt.

Passengers booking through to the North Station route change cars at the top of North Hill.

5 mins. service from top of North Hill to North Station from 5 p.m.

20

SUNDAYS.

From North Station.

To Lexden.

North Station depart.	Top of High Street depart.	Lexden arrive.
	9 10 a.m.	9 25 a.m.
	9 50	10 5
9 48 a.m.	9 55	
10 12	10 18	10 33
10 35	10 42	To depôt.
	12 20 p.m.	12 35 p.m.
	12 35	12 52
1 0 p.m.	1 7	1 24
1 30	1 37	1 54
2 0	2 7	2 24
2 29	2 35	2 50
	2 50	3 5
2 59	3 5	3 20
3 14	3 20	3 35

These times are repeated each hour of day, making a 15 minutes service to last cars, which run as follows :—

9 44 p.m.	9 50 p.m.	10 5 p.m.
9 59	10 5	To depôt.

21

SUNDAYS.

From North Station.

To Hythe.

North Station depart.	Top of High Street depart.	Hythe arrive.
9 55 a.m.	10 2 a.m.	
10 15	10 25	10 37 a.m.
10 25	10 32	10 46
	12 40 p.m.	12 54 p.m.
	1 10	1 24
	1 40	1 54
	2 10	2 24
	2 38	2 49
	2 50	3 4
	3 5	3 19
And every 15 minutes to—		
	4 20	4 34
	4 35	4 47
	4 48	5 1
	5 2	5 16
5 10 p.m.	5 17	5 31
And every 15 minutes to—		
9 40	9 47	10 1
9 55	10 2	To depôt.

22

SUNDAYS.

From North Station.

To Recreation Ground.

North Station depart.	Top of High Street depart.	Recreation Ground arrive.
10 0 a.m.	10 7 a.m.	
10 20	10 27	10 39 a.m.
12 42 p.m.	12 50 p.m.	1 3 p.m.
	1 16	1 25
1 41	1 46	1 55
2 11	2 16	2 25
2 41	2 46	2 55
	2 58	3 11
3 6	3 13	3 26
3 21	3 28	3 41
And every 15 minutes to—		
5 6	5 13	5 26
5 20	5 27	5 40
5 35	5 42	5 55
5 50	5 57	6 10
6 5	6 12	6 25
And every 15 minutes to—		
9 35	9 42	9 55
9 50	9 57	To depôt.

5 mins. service from North Station to top of North Hill from 5 p.m.

23

SUNDAYS.

From North Station.

To East Gates

North Station depart.	Top of High Street depart.	East Gates arrive.
10 10 a.m.	10 17 a.m.	
10 30	10 37	10 45 a.m.
	12 30 p.m.	12 39 p.m.
	12 50	12 59
	1 10	1 19

These times are repeated each hour of day, making a 20 minutes service to last car, which runs as follows :—

9 30 p.m.	9 39 p.m.

Passengers booking through from the North Station route to the East Gates route change cars at the top of North Hill.

5 mins. service from North Station to top of North Hill from 5 p.m.

24

WORKPEOPLE'S CARS.

Workpeople are allowed to travel at workpeople's fares on the following cars :—

MONDAYS TO THURSDAYS.

12.34 p.m. Hythe to High Street.
5.35 p.m. High Street to Lexden.
5.4 p.m. Hythe to North Station.
5.34 p.m. Hythe to North Station.
5.32 p.m. High Street to Hythe.
5.50 p.m. High St. to East Gates.
6.0 p.m. East Gates to High St.

FRIDAYS ONLY.

12.34 p.m. Hythe to High Street.
5.35 p.m. High Street to Lexden.
5.4 p.m. Hythe to North Station.
5.34 p.m. Hythe to North Station.
5.32 p.m. High Street to Hythe.
6.0 p.m. East Gates to High St.
6.10 p.m. High St. to East Gates.

SATURDAYS ONLY.

1.5 p.m. High Street to Lexden.
12.34 p.m. Hythe to North Station.
1.2 p.m. High Street to Hythe.
1.5 p.m. High St. to East Gates.

NOTE.—The above times are subject to alteration at the discretion of the Manager.

25

TRAMS FROM TOWN TO TERMINUS

Top Left: Tram 1 in St Botolphs Street bound for the Hythe amid a chaotic scene of two-way horse-drawn traffic. The modern scene is still very busy albeit now part of the town centre's one-way system.

Centre Left: Tram 2 in the rural charm of Lexden Road returns to town en-route to North Station with a well loaded top deck.

Top Right: Tram 3 in the High Street, a location much favoured by contemporary postcard suppliers. A fellow car-man waits by the tram stop for the vehicle bound for North Station.

Centre Right: Tram 4 at Hythe terminus with a young conductress posed in full length overcoat with bell punch, clippers, whistle and cash bag hung on two leather shoulder straps.

FIRST & LAST TRAM AT LEXDEN

Left: Tram 13 is seen on arrival at the Lexden terminus on 28 July 1904 driven by the Mayoress to inaugurate the tram system.

Right: Tram 16 prepares to return to the Car depot on 30 September 1928. The service was provided by Dennis motor buses the next day.

New Bus Routes

In March 1929 further new bus routes to Bergholt Road and Mile End were introduced and in November the Recreation Ground trams were supplemented by a St Botolphs - Old Heath bus service and a new service also commenced operation along Mersea Road to Middlewick. These new services saw the delivery of eight more Dennis buses giving a fleet total of 19 at the end of the year. On 8 December the last trams ran on the Recreation Ground and Hythe routes and the bus services, starting the next day, operated from Recreation Ground to North Station and Hythe to Mile End or Bergholt Road.

The Tramway Ends

This ended the operation of trams in Colchester with many trams being sold to Moss, a local building contractor for use as site huts at £5 each. Four survived into the early sixties, albeit without trucks, upper deck seating or trolley poles! The most complete example, tram no 13 of opening day fame, was offered to the Colchester Corporation Museum department but the Council were regrettably unable to accept the gift. Two others were burnt-out; one based on a farm at Rowhedge was filled with dry wood and hedge trimmings etc and cremated on Guy Fawkes night in 1962. The spectacle viewed from a distance appeared as though a building was on fire and some well meaning souls called out the already over-stressed fire brigade! Two hefty cast brackets that supported the canopy were fortunately saved as was the lower deck of tram no 10 by a keen tram preservationist at Walton-on-the-Naze. It is truly remarkable that anything of the system's stock should survive for 100 years.

The AEC era Commences

A change of supplier of buses came in May 1930 when three AEC Regents with Short Bros double deck bodies were purchased, and also an AEC Regal with locally built body by Harold Willett who had premises in the High Street where Williams & Griffin modern store now stands. Willett also converted the open top double deck Dennis vehicles to closed top in 1930.

The next bus route to commence, on 19 January 1931, was between Ipswich Road (St John's Church) and Maldon Road (Irvine Road) operating every half-hour. Further vehicles were purchased in December 1931 - a second Willett bodied AEC Regal and two AEC Regents with bodies built by Ransomes, Sims & Jefferies of Ipswich.

Competition Penalties

During the operation of the trams prior to 1929 the local bus operators charged fares 50% above those on the tram routes. When buses were introduced, the Corporation made an unsuccessful attempt to enforce protection by imposing a 25% levy on fares charged by other local operators to passengers picked up and set down within the Borough. In 1932 a further attempt was made to have the fares of other operators increased by 50% over those charged on Corporation buses but this was refused by the Traffic Commissioners.

All Routes Revised

The first major reorganisation of the bus services took place on 16 January 1933, the revised routes being as follows:

Service	Route	Basic weekday frequency
1	Parsons Heath - Butt Road (Drury Hotel)	20 minutes
2	Ipswich Road (St John's Church) - Shrub End (Leather Bottle)	30 minutes
3	Lexden (Clairmont Road or Borough Boundary) - North Station	15 minutes
4	Hythe - Mile End	15 minutes
5	Bergholt Road - Shrub End (Leather Bottle)	30 minutes
6	Old Heath - North Station	15 minutes
7	Mersea Road - High Street	30 minutes

This network remained very much unaltered until 1946 apart from the extension of service 5 to Dugard Avenue at Shrub End in March 1935, although timetables were subjected to many alterations particularly during the Second World War.

The opening of the new Colchester Bypass saw the introduction of a new circular service on 29 June 1933 which operated from High Street via Ipswich Road and along the Bypass (Cowdray Avenue, Colne Bank Avenue and Cymbeline Way) to Lexden and returning along Lexden Road to High Street every 40 minutes on Thursday, Saturday and Sunday afternoons and early evenings. This was really a circular tour which ran until 1 October and was repeated in 1934.

The last petrol engined buses to be delivered were three AEC Regents with Strachans bodywork in June 1936. Two of these buses (27, 28) gained the distinction of operating in London when they joined many other operators' buses on loan to LPTB during the London Blitz, operating from October 1940 to July 1941 being based at Seven Kings and Barking. On their return to Colchester, these buses carried suitable plaques on the lower deck bulkhead.

1: VW4389

An example of the first four of Colchester Corporation's motor buses delivered in May 1928, the Dennis G with neat Strachan & Brown 20 seat body is seen in Shrub End Road on delivery. The registration has still to be properly signwritten and sports a temporary chalked version. Some 68 years were to elapse before another normal control bus entered the fleet.

INITIAL MOTORBUS FLEET

5: VW 5125

A much larger version of the Dennis/Strachan & Brown combination came with the supply of five E models with 32 seat dual-entrance bodies. The brand new vehicle stands at the coachworks at Acton in North London in June 1928, again prior to the application of the sign written registration plate.

10: VW 6482

The first double-decker, again a Dennis/Strachan & Brown vehicle was one of a pair of H models with 48 seat open-top bodies. Seen in original form in Magdalen Street in September 1928, a roof and glazed windows were fitted by Willetts coachbuilders in Colchester High Street in 1930.

COLCHESTER CORPORATION OMNIBUS SERVICES.

PROVISIONAL TIME TABLE.

COMMENCING MAY 21st, 1928.

Weekdays.

Parsons Heath to Shrub End (Via MALDON ROAD)

Parsons Heath. Depart.	East-gates. Depart.	Town Hall. Depart.	Shrub End. Arrive.
a.m.	a.m.	a.m.	a.m.
7 45*	7 50*	7 56	8 12
8 15	8 20	8 26	8 42
8 45	8 50	8 56	9 12
9 15	9 20	9 26	9 42
9 45	9 50	9 56	10 12
10 15	10 20	10 26	10 42
10 45	10 50	10 56	11 12
11 15	11 20	11 26	11 42
11 45	11 50	11 56	12 12
p.m.	p.m.	p.m.	p.m.
12 15	12 20	12 26	12 42
12 50	12 56	1 2*	1 18
1 15†	1 20†	1 26	1 42
1 45†	1 50†	1 56	2 12
2 15	2 20	2 26	2 42
2 45	2 50	2 56	3 12
3 15	3 20	3 26	3 42
3 45	3 50	3 56	4 12
4 15	4 20	4 26	4 42
4 45	4 50	4 56	5 12
5 20	5 25	5 32†	5 48
5 45	5 50	5 56	6 12
6 15	6 20	6 26	6 42
6 45	6 50	6 56	7 12
7 15	7 20	7 26	7 42
7 45	7 50	7 56	8 12
8 15	8 20	8 26	8 42
8 45	8 50	8 56	9 12
9 15	9 20	9 26	9 42
9 45	9 50	9 56	10 12
10 15	10 20	10 26	To Depot.

Shrub End to Parsons Heath (Via MALDON ROAD)

Shrub End. Depart.	Town Hall. Depart.	East-gates. Depart.	Parsons Heath. Arrive.
a.m.	a.m.	a.m.	a.m.
7 49*	8 5	8 10	8 15
8 19	8 35	8 40	8 45
8 42	9 0	9 5	9 10
9 19	9 35	9 40	9 45
9 49	10 5	10 10	10 15
10 19	10 35	10 40	10 45
10 49	11 5	11 10	11 15
11 19	11 35	11 40	11 45
11 49	12 5pm	12 10pm	
p.m.	p.m.	p.m.	12 15
12 19	12 35*	12 40*	12 45
12 49	1 5	1 10	1 15
1 19	1 35	1 40	1 45
1 43†	2 0	2 5	2 10
2 19	2 35	2 40	2 45
2 49	3 5	3 10	3 15
3 19	3 35	3 40	3 45
3 49	4 5	4 10	4 15
4 19	4 35	4 40	4 45
4 49	5 5	5 10	5 15
5 19	5 35†	5 40†	5 45
5 49	6 5†	6 10†	6 15
6 19	6 35	6 40	6 45
6 49	7 5	7 10	7 15
7 19	7 35	7 40	7 45
7 49	8 5	8 10	8 15
8 19	8 35	8 40	8 45
8 49	9 5	9 10	9 15
9 19	9 35	9 40	9 45
9 49	10 5	10 10	10 15
10 12	10 28	To Depot.	

Weekdays.

Greenstead Road (Hythe Station Road) to Drury Hotel (Via BUTT ROAD)

Hythe Stat'n Rd. Depart.	East-gates. Depart.	Town Hall. Depart.	Drury Hotel. Arrive.
a.m.	a.m.	a.m.	a.m.
7 45*	7 47*	7 52	
8 1	8 5	8 10	8 15
8 31	8 35	8 40	8 45
9 1	9 5	9 10	9 15
9 31	9 35	9 40	9 45
10 1	10 5	10 10	10 15
10 31	10 35	10 40	10 45
11 1	11 5	11 10	11 15
11 31	11 35	11 40	11 45
p.m.	p.m.	p.m.	p.m.
12 1	12 5	12 10	12 15
12 31	12 35	12 40*	12 45
1 1	1 5	1 10	1 15
1 31	1 35	1 40	1 45
2 1	2 5	2 10	2 15
2 31	2 35	2 40	2 45
3 1	3 5	3 10	3 15
3 31	3 35	3 40	3 45
4 1	4 5	4 10	4 15
4 31	4 35	4 40	4 45
5 1	5 5	5 10	5 15
5 31	5 35	5 40†	5 45
6 1	6 5	6 10	6 15
6 31	6 35	6 40	6 45
7 1	7 5	7 10	7 15
7 31	7 35	7 40	7 45
8 1	8 5	8 10	8 15
8 31	8 35	8 40	8 45
9 1	9 5	9 10	9 15
9 31	9 35	9 40	9 45
10 1	10 5	10 10	10 15

Drury Hotel (Butt Road) to Hythe Station Road

Drury Hotel. Depart.	Town Hall. Depart.	East-gates. Depart.	Hythe Stat'n Rd. Arrive.
a.m.	a.m.	a.m.	a.m.
8 15*	8 20	8 25	8 29
8 45	8 50	8 55	8 59
9 15	9 20	9 25	9 29
9 45	9 50	9 55	9 59
10 15	10 20	10 25	10 29
10 45	10 50	10 55	10 59
11 15	11 20	11 25	11 29
11 45	11 50	11 55	11 59
p.m.	p.m.	p.m.	p.m.
12 15	12 20	12 25	12 29
12 45	12 50*	12 55*	12 59
1 15†	1 20	1 25	1 29
1 45	1 50	1 55	1 59
2 15	2 20	2 25	2 29
2 45	2 50	2 55	2 59
3 15	3 20	3 25	3 29
3 45	3 50	3 55	3 59
4 15	4 20	4 25	4 29
4 45	4 50	4 55	4 59
5 15	5 20	5 25	5 29
5 45	5 50	5 55	5 59
6 15	6 20	6 25	6 29
6 45	6 50	6 55	6 59
7 15	7 20	7 25	7 29
7 45	7 50	7 55	7 59
8 15	8 20	8 25	8 29
8 45	8 50	8 55	8 59
9 15	9 20	9 25	9 29
9 45	9 50	9 55	9 59
10 15	10 20	To Depot.	

FARES AND STAGES.

Fare Stage.		Fare—d.
PARSONS HEATH	to SHRUB END	4½
" "	to IRVINE ROAD	4
" "	to IRETON ROAD	3½
" "	to CREFFIELD ROAD	3
" "	to TOWN HALL	2½
" "	to BROOK STREET	2
" "	to EASTGATES	1½
" "	to FLYING FOX	1
FLYING FOX	to SHRUB END	4
" "	to IRVINE ROAD	3½
" "	to IRETON ROAD	3
" "	to CREFFIELD ROAD	2½
" "	to TOWN HALL	2
" "	to BROOK STREET	1½
" "	to EASTGATES	1
HYTHE STATION ROAD	to DRURY HOTEL	3
" " "	to HEADGATE	2½
" " "	to TOWN HALL	2
" " "	to BROOK STREET	1½
" " "	to EASTGATES	1
EASTGATES	to SHRUB END	3½
"	to IRVINE ROAD	3
"	to IRETON ROAD	2½
"	to WICKHAM ROAD	2½
"	to HEADGATE	2
"	to TOWN HALL	1½
"	to ALL SAINTS' CHURCH	1
BROOK STREET	to IRVINE ROAD	2½
" "	to DRURY HOTEL	2½
" "	to CREFFIELD ROAD	2
" "	to WICKHAM ROAD	2
" "	to HEADGATE	1½
" "	to TOWN HALL	1
ALL SAINTS' CHURCH	to IRETON ROAD	2
" " "	to DRURY HOTEL	2
" " "	to CREFFIELD ROAD	1½
" " "	to WICKHAM ROAD	1½
" " "	to HEADGATE	1
TOWN HALL	to SHRUB END	3
" "	to IRVINE ROAD	2
" "	to IRETON ROAD	1½
" "	to DRURY HOTEL	1½
" "	to CREFFIELD ROAD	1
" "	to WICKHAM ROAD	1
HEADGATE	to SHRUB END	2½
"	to IRVINE ROAD	1½
"	to IRETON ROAD	1
"	to DRURY HOTEL	1
CREFFIELD ROAD	to SHRUB END	2
" "	to IRVINE ROAD	1
IRETON ROAD	to SHRUB END	1½
IRVINE ROAD	to SHRUB END	1

TRANSFER STAGES.

PARSONS HEATH	to NORTH STATION	3½
FLYING FOX	to " "	3
HYTHE STATION ROAD	to " "	3
EASTGATES	to " "	2½
BROOK STREET	to " "	2
SHRUB END	to " "	3½
IRVINE ROAD	to " "	3
DRURY HOTEL	to " "	2½
IRETON ROAD	to " "	2½
WICKHAM ROAD	to " "	2
CREFFIELD ROAD	to " "	2

CHILDREN UNDER THREE YEARS OF AGE to be carried free.

CHILDREN OVER 3 AND UNDER 12 YEARS OF AGE to be charged half the adult fare. In the case of the fare being 1½d., 2½d., 3½d., 4½d., or 5½d., the half-fare will be reckoned as 1d., 1½d., 2d., 2½d., or 3d. respectively.

CHILDREN GOING TO AND FROM SCHOOL between the hours of 8 and 9.30 a.m., 12.0 and 2.30, and 3.30 and 6.0 p.m. to be allowed to travel at the reduced fare of 1d. between the Town Hall and any terminus.

WORKPEOPLE to be allowed to travel on workpeople's cars denoted on Timetables, at 1d. fare between the Town Hall and any terminus.

Sundays.

Parsons Heath to Shrub End (Via MALDON ROAD)

Parsons Heath. Depart.	East-gates. Depart.	Town Hall. Depart.	Shrub End. Arrive.
a.m.	a.m.	a.m.	a.m.
9 45	9 50	9 56	10 9
		10 20	10 35
10 40	10 45	10 51	11 3
11 25	11 30	11 36	11 48
p.m.	p.m.	p.m.	p.m.
12 10	12 15	12 20	12 32
12 53	12 58	1 3	1 15
1 37	1 42	1 47	1 59
2 21	2 26	2 31	2 43
2 45	2 50	2 56	3 12
3 15	3 20	3 26	3 42
3 45	3 50	3 56	4 12
4 15	4 20	4 26	4 42
4 45	4 50	4 56	5 12
5 15	5 20	5 26	5 42
5 45	5 50	5 56	6 12
6 15	6 20	6 26	6 42
6 45	6 50	6 56	7 12
7 15	7 20	7 26	7 42
7 45	7 50	7 56	8 12
8 15	8 20	8 26	8 42
8 45	8 50	8 56	9 12
9 15	9 20	9 26	9 42
9 45	9 50	9 56	10 12
10 15	10 20	10 26	To Depot

Shrub End to Parsons Heath (Via MALDON ROAD)

Shrub End. Depart.	Town Hall. Depart.	East-gates. Depart.	Parsons Heath. Arrive.
a.m.	a.m.	a.m.	a.m.
10 14	10 27	10 32	10 38
10 35	10 47		
11 3	11 15	11 20	11 25
		p.m.	p.m.
11 48	12 0	12 5	12 10
p.m.	p.m.		
12 32	12 44	12 49	12 53
1 15	1 27	1 32	1 37
1 59	2 11	2 16	2 21
2 19	2 35	2 40	2 45
2 49	3 5	3 10	3 15
3 19	3 35	3 40	3 45
3 49	4 5	4 10	4 15
4 19	4 35	4 40	4 45
4 49	5 5	5 10	5 15
5 19	5 35	5 40	5 45
5 49	6 5	6 10	6 15
6 19	6 35	6 40	6 45
6 49	7 5	7 10	7 15
7 19	7 35	7 40	7 45
7 49	8 5	8 10	8 15
8 19	8 35	8 40	8 45
8 49	9 5	9 10	9 15
9 19	9 35	9 40	9 45
9 49	10 5	10 10	10 15
10 12	10 28	To Depot.	

Sundays.

Greenstead Road (Hythe Station Road) to Drury Hotel (Via BUTT ROAD)

Hythe Stat'n Rd. Depart.	East-gates. Depart.	Town Hall. Depart.	Drury Hotel. Arrive.
a.m.	a.m.	a.m.	a.m.
10 0	10 4	10 9	10 14
11 1	11 5	11 10	11 15
11 31	11 35	11 40	11 45
p.m.	p.m.	p.m.	p.m.
12 1	12 5	12 10	12 15
12 31	12 35	12 40	12 45
1 1	1 5	1 10	1 15
1 31	1 35	1 40	1 45
2 1	2 5	2 10	2 15
2 31	2 35	2 40	2 45
3 1	3 5	3 10	3 15
3 31	3 35	3 40	3 45
4 1	4 5	4 10	4 15
4 31	4 35	4 40	4 45
5 1	5 5	5 10	5 15
5 31	5 35	5 40	5 45
6 1	6 5	6 10	6 15
6 31	6 35	6 40	6 45
7 1	7 5	7 10	7 15
7 31	7 35	7 40	7 45
8 1	8 5	8 10	8 15
8 31	8 35	8 40	8 45
9 1	9 5	9 10	9 15
9 31	9 35	9 40	9 45
10 1	10 5	10 10	10 15

Drury Hotel (Butt Road) to Hythe Station Road

Drury Hotel. Depart.	Town Hall. Depart.	East-gates. Depart.	Hythe Stat'n Rd Arrive.
a.m.	a.m.	a.m.	a.m.
10 14	10 20		
	10 47	10 52	10 57
11 15	11 20	11 25	11 29
11 45	11 50	11 55	11 59
p.m.	p.m.	p.m.	p.m.
12 15	12 20	12 25	12 29
12 45	12 50	12 55	12 59
1 15	1 20	1 25	1 29
1 45	1 50	1 55	1 59
2 15	2 20	2 25	2 29
2 45	2 50	2 55	2 59
3 15	3 20	3 25	3 29
3 45	3 50	3 55	3 59
4 15	4 20	4 25	4 29
4 45	4 50	4 55	4 59
5 15	5 20	5 25	5 29
5 45	5 50	5 55	5 59
6 15	6 20	6 25	6 29
6 45	6 50	6 55	6 59
7 15	7 20	7 25	7 29
7 45	7 50	7 55	7 59
8 15	8 20	8 25	8 29
8 45	8 50	8 55	8 59
9 15	9 20	9 25	9 29
9 45	9 50	9 55	9 59
10 15	10 20	To Depot.	

Passengers to be entitled to carry by hand, in the omnibuses, personal luggage, not of a bulky nature, up to 28 lbs. in weight. All other luggage not exceeding 56 lbs. in weight to be charged as follows :—Between Town Hall and any terminus 1d. per package, or 2d. per package through between any one terminus and another.

Dogs are not allowed on the Omnibuses.

NOTICE.—While exercising every care to insure the correct running of the Services, the Corporation will not be responsible for any irregularities which may occur

*Workpeople's Cars Mondays to Saturdays.
†Workpeople's Cars Mondays to Fridays.

W. H. SOULBY, M.Inst.T.,
General Manager.

May 1st, 1928.

The Essex County Telegraph, Printers, Colchester.

1929 DELIVERIES OUST THE TRAMS

Right: Tram 3 is posed with bus 11: VW6481 at North Station marking the replacement on the Lexden Road service of the electric powered trams running on steel wheels and track by quiet petrol powered bus mounted on pneumatic tyres. Centre Left: Bus 14: VW 8424 is seen when brand new at the Guildford premises of Dennis Bros. for a pre-delivery check in February 1929. One of a pair of H models, 14 was the first Colchester double-decker supplied new with closed top bodywork... by Strachan & Brown of course.

Centre Right: Bus 16: VX3224 was one of three of the more advanced Dennis HS (with a 5.7 litre engine on more flexible mountings, wider brake drums and a Dewandre servo unit) which completed the tram replacement programme. Seen at the North Station terminus bound for the Recreation Ground in Military Road with a conductor posed at the nearside. Bottom Right: Bus 18: VX2746 A pair of dual-door saloons were the last of the Dennis/Strachan monopoly. These were EV models with various mechanical improvements over the previous six E types. The brand new vehicle is seen prior to the application of the signwritten registration plates. Old Heath was served by service 6 not 7 as depicted!

AEC AEC were so pleased to gain an order from Colchester for three Regents (delivered in 1930 with bodies by Short Bros. of Rochester) that a photographer was commissioned to record the trio at work in the town.

Top left: 21: VX5552 climbs up North Hill, passing St Peter's Church as 23: VX5554 descends, clearly showing the exposed open staircase at the rear. Both buses are at work on service 6 (Old Heath to North Station).

Top Right: 22: VX5553 passing the Regal, later to be renamed The Odeon, (this closed by 2002 and was removed to the old Head Post Office in Head Street) bound for Clairmont Road via Lexden.

LOCAL BODYWORK

Centre 23: VX5554 was the first of a pair of Regals with bodies built by Harold Willett in a coachworks in the town's High Street, premises later occupied by William's (agricultural engineers) and in modern times, part of the Williams & Griffin department store. Some 39 years elapsed before the purchase of another single-decker, ironically an AEC.

Bottom: 25: EV3600 Delivered concurrently with the second Regal/Willett was a pair of AEC Regents with bodies by Ransomes, Sims & Jefferies of Ipswich, better known as manufacturers of trolleybuses and lawn mowers. 25 is seen at the Parsons Heath terminus outside Wents timber merchant yard in April 1947.   R.R.Eves.

Take-over Threat

In 1937, the Eastern National Omnibus Company again offered to operate the local bus services for a period of 21 years with a payment of £2000. The company would have acquired the vehicles and renewed them when necessary but the Corporation turned the offer down.

An unsuccessful Garrison Circular service was started on 19 September 1938 between High Street and Abbey Fields. Operating every 20 minutes on Monday to Saturdays between 9.30 a.m. and 9.30 p.m. (except 10.50 - 12.30 and 2.50 - 4.50 p.m.), the service only lasted until 11 February 1939.

Diesel Era Commences

The first diesel engined buses were delivered on 28 February 1939 in the form of five AEC Regents with Massey Brothers 52 seat bodywork. These were most attractive buses being fully lined out in gold on the tuscan red and cream livery. It is interesting to note that before their delivery a blue and white livery was considered presumably to relate to the local football club kit!

The fleet strength had reached 32 by 1939 and to accommodate the expansion a new garage (always referred to as No 2 Garage), adjacent to the tram shed, was opened in March, and included a paint shop to the rear. The garage was later extended to the rear beside the paint shop in 1958.

War Time

Colchester received a share of "utility" buses during the Second World War with 16 vehicles in the form of:

2	Bristol K5G, Bristol bodies	35/6
3	Guy Arab 5LW, Park Royal	37/8 and 45
2	Guy Arab 5LW, Weymann	39, 40
4	Guy Arab 5LW, Strachans	41-44
2	Bristol K6A, Duple	46/8
3	Bristol K6A, Park Royal	47/9 and 50

The first four had upholstered seats but the remainder were fitted with wooden slatted seats. During their lifetime the upholstered seats were removed and fitted to "younger" utility buses whilst others were fitted with upholstered seats from former London buses, all the wooden seats being removed by 1958.

Post War

Normal timetables were gradually restored from January 1944 with the standard timetable being reintroduced on 16 September 1945. A general "tidying-up" exercise took place on 4 March 1946 before major changes to services were introduced on 4 November 1946. The revised network was as follows:

Service	Route	Basic weekday frequency
1	Parsons Heath - Layer Road (Reed Hall Avenue)	15 minutes
2	Ipswich Road - Shrub End (Leather Bottle)	30 minutes
3	Ipswich Road - Lexden (Borough Boundary)	30 minutes
4	Hythe - Mile End* or Mill Road (Turner Road)	15 minutes
5	North Station - Head Street - Shrub End - Lexden	
	- Head Street - North Station (circular)	30 minutes
5A	North Station - Head Street - Lexden - Shrub End	
	- Head Street - North Station (circular)	30 minutes
6	Old Heath - North Station	15 minutes
7	Mersea Road - Bergholt Road	30 minutes

* Mile End buses were extended along Boxted Road to Severalls Hospital at certain times

Unique Bus

March/April 1947 saw the delivery of four AEC Regent IIs with Massey bodies but the more interesting vehicle arrived in November 1948 in the form of unique bus 55 - a Crossley DD42/2 with the 8.6 litre Crossley engine and torque converter. Massey bodywork was fitted but with slight differences to those on the AEC chassis. The bus was tested on non-PSV duties but the torque converter was removed before entering passenger service on 24 December 1948.

A new bus service commenced on 1 December 1947, operating a circular route from Head Street via East Hill, Greenstead Road, St Andrews Avenue, East Hill to Head Street. Numbered 8, service 8A operated the reverse route. Both routes ran every 30 minutes but patronage was low and the service was withdrawn the following year on 5 June.

LAST PETROL BUSES

Top: 27: DPU416 was the first of a trio of AEC Regent 661 with stylish lined out Strachans bodywork, seen in pristine condition when posed at the body manufacturers works at Acton prior to delivery to Colchester in July 1936.

Second from top: 28: DPU417, looking somewhat tired after 11 years service, is seen at the North Station terminus in June 1947 beside the "cattle-pens" (ineffective bus shelters), at work on service 5A to Clairmont Road via Lexden. The Colchester bodyshop staff had modified the rearmost window on the lower deck to Massey styling. R.R.Eves

Note: Buses 27 and 28 had the distinction of helping out in the blitzed metropolis both being loaned to the London Passenger Transport Board from October 1940 to July 1941. A plaque was affixed to the inside bulkhead as a token of the historic visit.

FIRST DIESEL BUSES

Second from bottom: 33 with 30: GVW949/946 Advancement into better reliability and greater economy came with the oil engine in March 1939 with the supply of five AEC Regent 0661 chassis with curvaceous bodywork by Massey Bros. of Wigan. These marked the beginning of a 30 year association with the Lancashire coachworks. The superb pair are posed at the AEC works at Southall prior to delivery.

Bottom: 30: GVW946 Still in fine fettle having survived the lean war years, the bus is little changed from new, apart from acquiring a red roof and losing the elaborate lining out and flamboyant fleet numbers after 16 years service and several repaints. Seen waiting time in Mile End Road opposite the Railway Hotel stable block bound for Hythe Quay in April 1955.
GR Mills

Corporation Transport Department.

NOTICE TO PASSENGERS.

9 P.M. BUSES FROM TOWN TO EACH TERMINUS.

The Transport Committee has decided that if **AIR RAID** danger is imminent at the time the Buses are due to leave the Garage, the above services will be suspended until immediate danger is past.

If danger is still imminent at 9.30 p.m. the services will be Cancelled.

Corporation Transport Offices,
Magdalen Street.

W. H. SOULBY, M. Inst. T.,
General Manager.

B. V. Ward, Printer, Colchester

Above right:- A preserved Colchester Corporation Transport bus stop and timetable frame.

PUBLICITY from the PAST

DIAMOND JUBILEE Celebrations 1904 - 64

DECORATED BUS

Colchester Corporation Transport Department

During the period 3rd to 11th October, 1964 (inclusive) a DECORATED BUS will operate throughout the day on each service as follows:

Saturday	3rd October		Service	1 and 1A
Sunday	4th	,,	,,	2 and 2A
Monday	5th	,,	,,	3
Tuesday	6th	,,	,,	4
Wednesday	7th	,,	,,	5 and 5A
Thursday	8th	,,	,,	5A and 5
Friday	9th	,,	,,	6
Saturday	10th	,,	,,	7
Sunday	11th	,,	,,	7

Ordinary Fares will be charged

Transport Offices
Magdalen Street
Colchester
28th September, 1964

J. GRAY
General Manager

E.T.P., COL.

16

"UNFROZEN"

35: JPU581 Production of buses ceased in 1941; but eventually authorisation controlled by the Ministry of War Transport was gained to complete vehicles that had been in the course of construction. These were known as "unfrozen" buses and two were allocated to Colchester. Completely non-standard, the pair introduced Bristols with Gardner engines into the fleet in June 1942. Nine Guys with same power unit followed in 1943/44. The bus presents a brave sight in the High Street bound for Severalls Mental Hospital.

IN FOR THE NIGHT GUYS ☾

42, 41, 44, 39, 43, Bristols 46 and 48, one of the Bristol/Park Royals 47/9/50 and unfrozen 36 are seen in Magdalen Street garage in April 1960.   G.R.Mills

GLOOMY WARTIME

45: JVW242 The first of the Arab II types, a Park Royal bodied example, was supplied with the usual cream band below the lower deck windows whereas the subsequent Strachans and Weymann deliveries were devoid of this feature (see the line up in the picture above). In full wartime guise, with white edged wings and hooded headlamps, 45 is seen loading a queue of American airmen from nearby Boxted airfield at the Ipswich Road turn. Brickhouse Farm, owned by Colchester Borough, and a police beacon in the background are worthy of note.

GUY ARAB 5LW – CHOICE OF BODYWORK

PARK ROYAL

38: JTW750 was one of a pair of Arab I models which benefited from a shorter bonnet line and hence a neater frontal treatment as portrayed; this, together with the wide cream band made this pair more stylish than their successors. Seen passing St Peters Church on North Hill en-route to Old Heath Post Office (a short working of service 6). The British Rail 1949 Karrier Bantam 2 ton articulated unit at the rear is particularly worthy of note.

WEYMANN

39: JTW982 was one of a pair with bodywork built at Addlestone, Surrey. These were the first utilities delivered with wooden slatted seats, a style which had been expelled from the fleet with the passing of the tramcars. Seen at Bardfield Road on Monkwick housing estate in August 1959, a regular haunt of the type from April 1953.   G.R.Mills

STRACHANS

43: JVW581 was still going very strong, 18 years to the day after entry into service, when seen in Sheepen Road passing the North East Essex Technical College in May 1962. Withdrawn four months later, 43 was the last of nine Arabs to see service in Colchester.   G.R.Mills

REQUIEM TO ALL THE GOOD GUYS THAT HAVE GONE! ... 42 YEARS AGO

Top right: I ain't got nobody! 38: JTW750 reduced to a chassis for instructional purposes at the Motor Vehicle section of the Engineering Department at the NE Essex Technical College in Sheepen Road seen during April 1959. 5 cylinder Gardner engine well exposed.

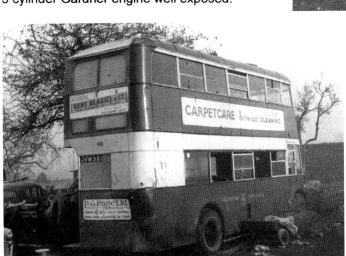

Above right: 37: JTW749 served the town for 16 years and ended its days at the Coggeshall Road, Earls Colne scrap yard and operational depot of S. Blackwell and Sons in July 1965. Famed as an operator of a daily Halstead to London express service and a daily Halstead to Colchester stage service. Furthermore the same business had offered to run the town's bus services back in 1927.

Top left and bottom left:
43: JVW581 the last of nine Arabs which totalled over 18 years service to the town. See page 18 for the Guy at work in Sheepen Road (location of the chassis of 38 as seen top right!). The final journey was only a few hundred yards to Saunders Carter compound in Magdalen Street, which was formerly part of the coal storage areas of St Botolph's station goods yard.   G.R.Mills (4)

RANSOMES SIMS & JEFFERIES, LTD.

DIRECTORS
Sir REUBEN HUNT, Chairman
G. PAWLYN, Deputy Chairman
H. H. DAWSON
G. B. W. SCHOLEFIELD
W. A. HUNT
W. D. ARESTER
Sir JOHN GREAVES, C.B.E.
J. S. CANNING

OUR REF LTO/BL

IPSWICH
ENGLAND

LONDON OFFICE
59 OLD BROAD STREET, E.C.2.

YOUR REF

TELEPHONES
ORWELL WORKS, IPSWICH 54711 (8 Lines)
SPARES SERVICE, IPSWICH 54713/4
NACTON WORKS, IPSWICH 76811
TELEGRAMS
"RANSOMES, IPSWICH, TELEX"
TELEX
TELEX No.1874

DATE 16th April

STRACHANS
SUCCESSORS LTD

COACHBUILDERS AND ENGINEERS
REGISTERED OFFICE
WALES FARM ROAD AND VICTORIA ROAD · NORTH ACTON · LONDON · W.3.
WORKS OPPOSITE NORTH ACTON STATION (CENTRAL LONDON RAILWAY)

ALL CORRESPONDENCE TO BE
ADDRESSED TO THE COMPANY
AND NOT TO INDIVIDUALS

DIRECTORS
E.E. STRACHAN
GEO. RAE
E.H.F. BULLARD

OUR REF. EJA/EMG
YOUR REF.

TELEPHONE
ACORN 0033
(3 lines)

TELEGRAPHIC
ADDRESS
STROBUS, WESPHONE
LONDON

CONTRACTORS TO H.M. Government

TELEPHONE WIGAN 82219   TELEGRAMS MASSEY BROS. WIGAN

Massey Brothers
(Pemberton) Limited
COACHBUILDERS

DIRECTORS: A. TYLDESLEY, A.M.I.E.E.
C. TYLDESLEY

SINGLE & DOUBLE DECK OMNIBUSES
TROLLEY BUSES, LUXURY COACHES

ENFIELD STREET
WIGAN

YOUR REF.   OUR REF.

P.R.V. GROUP BODY SALES DIVISION
PARK ROYAL VEHICLES LTD.
ABBEY ROAD, PARK ROYAL,
LONDON, N.W.10.
THE SELLING ORGANISATION FOR
PARK ROYAL VEHICLES LTD.   CHARLES H. ROE LTD.

TELEPHONE:
ELGAR 6522 (10 Lines)

TELEGRAMS:
KOACHWORKS,
HARLES, LONDON

YOUR REF   OUR REF ALC/MF.

Top: 25: EV3600 AEC Regent seen prior to delivery posed at Foxhall Heath, in October 1931. RS&J Ltd were well known manufacturers of lawn mowers and trolleybuses.

Above left: 27: DPU416 AEC Regent seen posed up at the chassis manufacturers works at Southall prior to delivery in July 1936. The stylish lining out and cream top was not perpetuated on repaints.

Lower left: 31: GVW947 AEC Regent. One of the first of five diesel buses. See page 15 for the illustrations of 33 brand new and 30 when 16 years old.

Bottom: 37: JTW749 Guy Arab seen when brand new in Magdalen Street May 1943. Note: white-edged wings, hooded headlamps, the lack of fleet name and the route number box under the canopy.

A FINE PAIR OF BRISTOLS

46: KEV331
47: KEV624

Both 1945 Bristol K6A chassis but with different bodybuilders. Ironically this pair outlived the other three of the type.

Top: 46 prepares to pass 47 at St John's Green on a PSV Circle farewell tour to the breed.

Middle: 46 ahead of 47 in Dugard Avenue near the junction with Parr Drive, seen during May 1962. 46 is on a short working of service 1 to High Street, 47 is on service 5.

47: KEV624 stands outside no 2 Garage having run in dead from Lexden Church. Emerging from the depot ... bus 46 prepares to reverse in having worked on service 3 from St Andrews Avenue whilst one of the four Crossleys waits to be refuelled and cleaned after working service 2 into High Street. An evening scene in July 1962.

GR Mills (3)

POST-WAR STOCK

51: KPU515 was one of four AEC Regents with the familiar, curvaceous, Massey body. The bus was hired by Osbornes of Tollesbury for the Colchester meeting of the PSV Circle and is seen in the unfamiliar location of Abberton reservoir en-route to Tollesbury via Birch in October 1965 while on a farewell to the class, which was withdrawn by February 1966.

52: KPU516 The severe winter of 1962/63 took its toll on the rolling stock – the large radiators froze at the bottom while the top tanks boiled. 52 is seen at work on service 5 to Dugard Avenue but has turned into the undeveloped Norman Way, off Lexden Road, to await rescue during January 1963.

NB. PSV Licence discs for bus 52 see page 84

UNIQUE 55
55: KPU519

The only Crossley ever fitted with a Massey body. Originally fitted with a radiator with the Maltese cross motif on it, 55 had the later Crossley badge when seen by the Drury Hotel in Layer Road bound for Homefield Road on St Michaels Estate in September 1961. Note the gleaming Triumph Mayflower on the pub forecourt in the background.

GR Mills (3)

Bus Order Change

The next delivery of new buses in 1949 saw yet another change of suppliers. Five Daimler CVD6s with bodies built by Charles Roberts Ltd of Wakefield arrived in March and April. Fleetnumbers reverted to 1 - 5 for these new buses which had preselector gearboxes which from time to time caused drivers considerable pain! i.e. if the operating pedal was not fully depressed, it would return with such force as to injure the drivers shin. A further five similar buses were ordered but the Corporation was refused loan sanction so four were delivered to Accrington Corporation and one to independent Brown's Blue of Markfield, Leicestershire, which later served with Ronsway of Hemel Hempstead, Hertfordshire. However a small part of these buses did come to Colchester in the form of the rear destination and route number boxes which were fitted into the rear of some of the utility Guys. It is pleasing to record that 4 (OHK432) has now been beautifully restored and is kept in the Lincolnshire Vintage Vehicle Society collection. When viewed, it is hard to believe that this bus is now fifty-five years old.

Further changes were made to services in 1949. In April some journeys on service 1 were extended to the military corrective establishment at Berechurch Camp. On 22 May the Shrub End and Lexden routes were changed again and the circulars (5/5A) were replaced: Service 2 was extended to Dugard Avenue at Shrub End and increased to every 15 minutes; service 3 was withdrawn; and service 5 was revised to operate every 15 minutes between North Station and Lexden with alternate journeys running to Dugard Avenue or the Borough Boundary. From the same date all the Mile End journeys on service 4 ran to Severalls Hospital.

A new circular works service, mainly for employees of E N Mason & Sons Ltd commenced on 2 December 1950 between High Street, North Hill, Cowdray Avenue, East Hill and High Street. Buses showed 3 or 3A on the number blinds but for some reason these numbers were not shown in the timetable booklet until 1959.

Ticket Update

Bell Punch type tickets, which had originally been used on the trams, with place names and subsequently with fare stage numbers were replaced by five value Ultimate ticket machines in the year ending March 1950. Ticket rolls were supplied by Punch & Ticket Co Ltd. This system continued until 1965 when TIM machines and tickets were introduced.

Petrol Power Ousted

A further change of vehicles came in 1951 with the delivery of two all-Crossley buses followed by two similar vehicles in 1952. These saw the end of petrol-engined buses with the withdrawal of AEC Regents 28 and 29 (DPU 417/8) in November 1952.

The development of Colchester with large council house building in the Shrub End and Mersea Road areas was catered for by the extension of services and increased frequencies. On 13 August 1951 service 1 was extended beyond Reed Hall Avenue to John Kent Avenue with some journeys extended from September further to Homefield Road, a military housing development. The frequency of service 2 along Shrub End Road was increased at peak times between High Street and the Leather Bottle. From 12 April 1953, the service along Mersea Road was doubled with the introduction of buses to the Monkwick estate as service 7 was revised to run between Head Street and Blackheath (Cherry Tree) or Monkwick (Queen Elizabeth Way). The utility Guys were regular performers on this route. Other changes from the same date saw all journeys on service 4 diverted along Mill Road to Defoe Crescent and the extension of service 5 alternately to Bergholt Road and via Turner Road, Defoe Crescent to Severalls (the latter journeys were subsequently numbered 5A from 16 August).

Additional early morning journeys were introduced on all routes from 7 September 1953 so as to provide arrivals in the Town Centre at about 7.00 a.m. instead of 7.45.

In February 1953 a new "Essex" bus washing machine was installed in No 2 Garage. Sunday morning was the main "bath-day" and it was a common sight to see a long row of buses parked along Magdalen Street having been put out to dry because of restricted space within the garages.

An increase in the fleet from 35 to 38 buses came with the delivery of three AEC Regent IIIs with Massey bodies in the autumn of 1953. The undertaking's Golden Jubilee was celebrated in 1954 and Crossley 9 was painted in a special cream livery and decorated with flags and illuminations and ran on each route during one week in October. The bus retained the livery until repaint in March 1957.

A minor re-routing at Lexden from 17 January 1954 saw service 5A buses diverted along Halstead Road and King Coel Road to avoid reversing off the busy London Road at the "Borough Boundary" terminus.

Monkwick develops

The development of the Monkwick housing estate continued fairly rapidly with various alterations being made to service 7 as follows:
23 May 1954 - Monkwick journeys extended to Bardfield Road.
3 April 1955 - Cherry Tree journeys diverted via Stansted Road and Queen Elizabeth Way.
19 June 1955 - Bardfield Road journeys re-routed via the whole length of Monkwick Avenue.

23

DAIMLER DYNASTY

In for the night during June 1960, 1 - 5 are parked up in No 2 garage but not in numerical order. The late shift yard shunters have 2/1/4/5/3 in the line. The only symmetry is the "book ends" which have painted radiator shells while the centre three have the original chromed ones.

3: OHK431 is seen at Headgate in September 1961 before the one-way which only permits travel in the opposite direction to the bus. This scene typifies Colchester in the sixties with the policeman on point duty overriding the traffic lights, a soldier with kit bag over his shoulder (the town has had a military presence since Roman times) and Head Street grid-locked with traffic (no change over 40 years later!).

1: OHK429 was the only one of the five Robert's bodied Daimlers to receive the experimental "layer" cake livery and is seen passing the cemetery in Mersea Road in February 1966 two days before withdrawal from service. The bus is bound for Bardfield Road, Monkwick to take up a peak hour extra journey.

GR Mills (3)

THE CROSSLEY QUARTET

Top right: 6: SVW451 works the first service journey into Prettygate on Sunday 12 October 1958 prior to Hills builders creating the Shopping Centre and housing estate. The Chief Inspector, Tom Stafford, leans on a pre-war Morris 8.   RN Collins

Top left: Bus 6 is seen at the revised Prettygate terminus at Hills Crescent West during September 1966 in an experimental revised livery which was not adopted as standard. Centre left: 7: SVW452, seen in John Kent Avenue in February 1967, sports another experimental livery which was adopted. Centre right: 9: TVX497, painted cream to celebrate the Golden Jubilee of operations in the Borough, is seen in Mile End Road (North Station stop) in April 1955 devoid of flags and external illuminations. Bus 9 was repainted back into standard livery in March 1957 (as no 8 in the picture below). Bottom: 6, 7: SVW451/2 and 8: TVX496 displaying all three livery variants are posed on Sheepen Road to mark the impending withdrawal of the unique Crossley/Massey 55.   All five Colchester Crossleys were paraded for the local PSV Circle membership on 24 September 1967.   G.R.Mills (4)

10: WPU732 was one of a trio of nicely proportioned Massey-bodied AEC Regent IIIs although somewhat rare with crash gearboxes and 7.7 litre engines. Seen in April 1962 freshly repainted at the Bergholt Road terminus at Braiswick. In the background is Woods (fan manufacturers) Sports Ground which, by the new millennium was a housing development.

LAST OF THE EXPOSED RADIATOR TRADITIONALS

11: WPU733 is seen on a bleak, traffic free, St Andrews Avenue beside the by-pass bound for Barnhall on the hourly service 3. A heavy mist hangs over the town in this January 1967 view and there a few brave passengers aboard the unheated bus. Baughans, the advertisers, had provisions shops in Wyre Street, Colchester and branches at Braintree, Chelmsford and Clacton, all now gone.

10-12: WPU 732-4 Three of a kind, all posed up for a farewell trip for the PSV Circle's Colchester meeting in October 1970 on Sheepen Road car park. Although in good order, the advent of OMO and front entrance/rear-engined buses considerably reduced their commercial value and regrettably these three fine buses were scrapped a year later.

GR Mills (3)

Shrub End Develops

In the south-west of the town the Shrub End estate was also developing fast and on 19 December 1954 service 1 buses to John Kent Avenue were extended into the estate to terminate at Hedge Drive. On service 2 the local daytime journeys terminating at the Leather Bottle were diverted from Shrub End Road via Walnut Tree Way to Owen Ward Close and renumbered 2A. On 5 December 1955 services 2A and 7 were linked, the new through service from Monkwick or Cherry Tree via the Town Centre to Shrub End (Owen Ward Close) being numbered 7.

Earlier on 3 April 1955, the Mile End services were revised again to improve reliability, the altered routes being:

4	Hythe - Bergholt Road
4A	Hythe - Mill Road via Turner Road
5	Dugard Avenue - Turner Road via Mile End Road
5A	Lexden (Borough Boundary) - Severalls via Mile End Road and Defoe Crescent

The Regent V Era

Three years elapsed before any more new buses were taken into stock in 1956 with the introduction of Massey 61-seat bodies which were to be the standard for the next ten years. The first four AEC Regent Vs were delivered in August and September. Unfortunately 16 (682HEV) suffered a front end accident with a motor-cycle at Parsons Heath on its first day in service but it was soon repaired at a cost of £122.9s.2d (£122.46).

These new buses saw the withdrawal of the first wartime buses including Bristol K5G no 36 which had also been involved in an accident with a motor-cycle on Lexden Hill. It had been proposed to convert the bus to a training and towing vehicle but this was never completed and it was eventually sold in 1961.

Tours

Sunday evening circular tours of the town over four different routes were operated from 6 May to 26 August 1956 using the Daimlers and again from 5 May to 25 August 1957 but total receipts were only £119 in 1956 and £68 in 1957 so the Transport Committee decided not to operate them in 1958.

Crisis

Fuel rationing caused by the Suez Crisis in 1956 resulted in reduced timetables being operated on Monday - Thursday evenings and on Sundays between 17 December 1956 and 8 April 1957. This had a "knock on" effect with the introduction of permanent reductions to Monday to Friday evening and Sunday timetables from 16 February 1958.

The development of the Monkwick estate had now spread south of Berechurch Hall Road and so the Bardfield Road journeys on service 7 were extended to Finchingfield Way from 19 May 1957 but these were cut back to Gosfield Road from 1 September due to difficulties with parked cars.

By-Pass and Prettygate served

The provision of a bus service along the Colchester By-pass (Cowdray Avenue and St Andrews Avenue) had been given consideration from time to time and eventually on 1 September 1958 the resident's requests were met by diverting one bus an hour off service 5 to St Andrews Avenue (near Greenstead Road), these journeys being numbered 3. Unfortunately these journeys omitted to serve North Station.

Another new housing development (council and private) was started in 1958 in the Lexden and Shrub End area on the site of Prettygate Farm and to serve this alternate journeys on service 7 were re-routed via King Harold Road to terminate at what would become Prettygate Shopping centre, from 12 October 1958. The evening and Sunday journeys on service 2 to and from the Leather Bottle were also re-routed to Prettygate and incorporated into service 7.

Returns

For many years there had been a system of issuing return tickets valid at peak times for the benefit of work people at a flat fare. In 1933 the fare was 2d (less than 1p) but this had reached 6d (2½p) by 1958. After much deliberation these return tickets were no longer issued after 10 November 1958 although the Traffic Commissioner recommended that some form of concession should continue. It was to be a year later, on 23 November 1959, when books of discounted tickets were sold but these were never popular with passengers or staff because of the need to issue a no-value exchange ticket and the concession was finally withdrawn in February 1971.

TIM Tickets

BIGGER BUSES

The eleven AEC Regent V/Massey introduced 61 seaters to the fleet; the largest then operated.

Top: 16: 682HEV, one of the first batch of four, is seen (left) in original livery turning at Welshwood Park Road, Parsons Heath in January 1965; and (right) in experimental rosy-red livery approaching the Albert roundabout in North Station Road in August 1974 as fleet number 60. Centre left: 5 (ex 15) 681HEV was the Transport department's first dedicated training bus. Painted bright orange it is seen in action at Kingsford Cross Roads in Layer Road during April 1976. Centre right: 20: 1298F was one of the second batch of four and is seen amid the winter snow of January 1967 turning out of Egerton Green Road on the Shrub End Estate.

Above right: 21: 193MNO, one of the final trio, received a minor livery variation when the centre roof panels were painted silver as an insulation test experiment, and is seen in Hawthorn Avenue in June 1965. The then barren land in the background became an extension of the Greenstead housing estate. Bottom right: 22: 194MNO was chosen to be decorated for the Diamond Jubilee with flags and illuminations and is seen at the Cherry Tree terminus in Mersea Road in October 1964. As the sign shows, the turn is very close to the borough boundary.

GR Mills (6)

Routes relinked

With a view to more economical operation and to ease some of the more arduous running times a major revision of services took place on 13 September 1959 which involved relinking the cross town routes and reducing frequencies so that, in general, the basic Monday to Friday timetable was every 20 minutes on each route. This had the unfortunate effect of only providing a 40 minute frequency on the outer "legs" of some routes. On Saturdays, services ran every 15 minutes between about 8.00 a.m. and 6.00 p.m. but this involved a considerable amount of overtime being worked and the services became unreliable particularly during the afternoon and evening. The revised routes were:

Service	Route
1/1A	Parsons Heath - Dugard Avenue or Prettygate
2/2A	Ipswich Road - Severalls or Mill Road
3	Town Centre - St Andrews Avenue (hourly)
4	Hythe - Layer Road Estate or Berechurch Camp
5/5A	Lexden (Dugard Avenue or Borough Boundary) - Bergholt Road or Turner Road
6	Old Heath - Prettygate or Shrub End Estate
7	North Station - Mersea Road or Monkwick Estate

From the same date the terminus at Parsons Heath was moved from St Johns Road further along to a new junction at Welshwood Park Road as this was considered to be a less dangerous reversing point despite the close proximity of the railway bridge on a bend.

These changes to timetables were not well received by passengers and resulted in an overall reduction in ridership and revenue. As an interim measure, the duplication at peak times on services 6 and 7 was rescheduled from 22 August 1960 to provide 10 minute frequencies between High Street and Old Heath Post Office and to Monkwick (Bardfield Road), but the council resolved that the original frequencies be restored. Consequently revised timetables providing a 15 minute frequency during the day on Mondays to Fridays, similar to those applying on Saturdays, were introduced from 30 January 1961. This did not apply to service 3 and the revised cross town links were retained.

The reversing of buses at the Straight Road/Dugard Avenue junction was discontinued on 14 July 1960 when the terminus was moved to Parr Drive in Dugard Avenue. This was still a reversing movement and unfortunately accidents continued to occur.

Leylands introduced

The 1960 order for five new buses resulted in a surprising change of chassis supplier. The specification still required 7ft 6ins wide buses which AEC no longer produced. Consequently the order was placed with Leyland Motors Ltd for five PD2/31 models with the rather unattractive front end. However Massey bodywork was supplied. Bus 28 (9671VX) was also fitted with power assisted steering - the first vehicle of this type to be so equipped but some years later it was removed.

Further deliveries of new buses in 1963/64 were also of Leyland manufacture but with the more attractive "St Helens" style fibre glass front end. The Massey bodies also featured fluorescent lighting throughout. In 1966 Colchester reluctantly changed to 8ft wide vehicles and AEC once again submitted a tender but the order was placed with Leyland for six PD2A/30 chassis with Massey 61-seat bodies.

A minor route alteration at Old Heath was introduced on 21 May 1961 when outward buses were diverted via Wick Road to reach the terminus at Speedwell Road.

Greenstead served

The new development to the east of the town between Harwich Road and St Andrews Avenue was first served from 18 June 1961 when alternate journeys on services 1/1A to and from Parsons Heath were re-routed at "The Royal Oak" via Bromley Road, Hawthorn Avenue and Sycamore Road to Laburnum Grove on the Greenstead estate. There were less than 200 homes occupied at the time but this development grew rapidly over the next few years.

Station served

Colchester's main line station, known locally as North Station (but never by the train operators) was rebuilt during 1961 with a much enlarged approach on the down side. At the request of British Railways a scheme was prepared for all buses serving North Station to be diverted along the approach road to the new station entrance and from 1 October the scheme commenced. Subsequently British Railways advised they intended to charge ½d (0.2p) per visit but the Transport Committee refused to pay. However part of the road then collapsed and all buses were withdrawn from 16 January 1962. Many complaints had been received from Mile End passengers that it was often a waste of time for all buses to use the Approach Road and when the road was repaired only terminating buses on service 7 were reinstated from 23 April. The question of the fee was not resolved at the time.

COLCHESTER CORPORATION TRANSPORT

FARE TABLE

Commencing Monday, 1st April, 1963

Service 1 GREENSTEAD ESTATE—SHRUB END
Service 1A PARSONS HEATH—PRETTYGATE

Stage No.		
8		Almond Way or Welshwood Park Road
7	2	Bromley Road
6	3 2	Flying Fox
5	3 3 2	Dilbridge Road
4	4 3 2 2	East Gates
3	5 4 3 3 2	Brook Street
2	6 5 4 4 3 2	Bus Stn. (Queen St.) or Holly Trees Museum
2	6 5 5 4 4 3 2	Osborne Street
1	6 5 5 4 4 3 2 2	Vineyard St. or Head St. or High St.
2	7 6 5 5 4 4 3 3 2	Creffield Road
3	8 7 6 6 5 5 4 4 3 2	Cambridge Road
4	8 8 7 6 6 5 4 4 4 3 2	Drury Road
5	9 9 8 7 7 6 5 5 5 4 3 2	Walnut Tree Way
6	10 9 9 8 8 7 6 6 6 5 4 3 2	Leather Bottle
7	11 10 10 9 9 8 7 7 7 6 5 4 3 2	Dugard Avenue
6	10 9 8 8 7 7 6 6 5 4 3 2 2 –	Hastings Road
7	10 10 9 9 8 7 7 7 6 5 4 3 2 – 2	Prettygate Shopping Centre
8	10 10 9 9 8 8 7 7 6 5 4 4 3 – 2 2	Hills Crescent West

Service 2 IPSWICH ROAD—SEVERALLS
Service 2A IPSWICH ROAD—MYLAND HOSPITAL

Stage No.		
10		Betts' Factory
9	2	Severalls Lane
8	3 2	Myland Hall Chase
7	4 3 2	Goring Road
6	4 4 3 2	Dilbridge Road
5	5 4 3 2 2	Ipswich Road Junction
4	6 5 4 3 2 2	Brook Street
3	7 6 5 4 3 3 2	Bus Station (Queen Street)
3	7 6 5 4 4 3 3 2	Osborne Street
2	7 6 5 4 4 3 3 2 2	Vineyard Street
2	7 6 5 4 3 3 2 – – –	Holly Trees Museum
1	7 6 5 4 4 3 3 3 3 2 2	Head St. or High St.
2	7 7 6 5 5 4 3 3 3 2 2 2	Middleborough
3	8 7 6 5 5 4 4 4 4 3 3 2 2	Colne Bank Avenue
4	8 8 7 6 6 5 4 4 4 4 4 3 2 2	North Station
5	9 9 8 7 7 6 5 5 5 5 5 4 3 3 2	Mile End Road
6	10 10 9 8 7 7 6 6 6 5 5 5 4 4 3 2	Dog and Pheasant
7	11 10 9 8 8 7 7 7 7 6 6 6 5 4 4 3 2	Defoe Cresc. Centre or Turner Rd.
8	11 11 10 9 9 8 8 7 7 7 7 7 6 5 5 4 3 2	Severalls
8	11 11 10 9 9 8 8 8 8 7 7 7 6 5 5 4 3 2	Myland Hospital

SCHOOL CHILDREN'S FARE: St. Helena School—Severalls—North Station, 2½d.

Service 3 BARNHALL ESTATE—ST. ANDREWS AVENUE

Stage No.		
8		Meopham Court
7	2	Unity Close
6	3 2	Barnhall Ave. Jct. or Scarletts Rd.
5	3 3 2	Recreation Ground
4	4 3 3 2	Camp Church
3	5 4 4 3 2	St. Botolph's Stn. or Osborne St.
2	5 5 4 3 3 2	Bus Stn. (Queen St.)
2	5 5 4 3 3 2 2	Holly Trees Museum
2	5 5 4 3 3 2 – –	Vineyard Street
1	6 5 5 4 4 3 3 2 2	Head St. or High St.
2	6 6 5 4 4 3 3 2 2 2	Middleborough
3	7 6 6 5 5 4 4 3 3 2 2	Colne Bank Avenue
4	8 7 7 6 5 4 4 4 4 3 3 2	Arclight Works
5	9 8 8 7 6 5 5 5 5 4 4 3 2	Lamp-post 16 or 17 Cowdray Avenue
6	9 8 8 7 7 6 6 5 5 5 4 4 3 2	St. Andrews Ave. (Ipswich Rd. Roundabout)
7	10 9 9 8 8 7 7 6 6 6 5 4 3 2 2	Telephone Box
8	10 10 10 9 8 7 7 7 7 7 6 5 4 3 3 2	202–206 St. Andrews Avenue

Service 3A TOWN CENTRE—ARCLIGHT WORKS—TOWN CENTRE (Circular)

Stage No.		
1		Head Street or High Street
2	2	Middleborough
3	2 2	Colne Bank Avenue
4	3 3 2	Arclight Works
5	4 4 3 2	Lamp-post 16 or 17 Cowdray Avenue
6	5 4 4 3 2	St. Andrews Avenue (Ipswich Rd. Roundabout)
5	5 5 4 3 2 2	Ipswich Road Junction
4	6 5 4 3 2 2 2	Brook Street
3	7 6 5 4 3 3 3 2	Bus Station (Queen Street)
3	7 7 6 5 4 4 3 3 2	Osborne Street
2	7 7 6 5 4 4 3 3 2 2	Vineyard Street
2	7 6 5 4 3 3 3 2 – – –	Holly Trees Museum
1	7 7 6 5 4 4 3 3 3 3 2 2	Head St. or High St.

Service 4 HYTHE—LAYER ROAD ESTATE or BERECHURCH CAMP

Stage No.		
7		Hawkins Road
6	2	Hythe Quay or Paxman's (Port Lane)
5	3 2	Port Lane
4	3 2 2	Wimpole Road
3	4 3 3 2	St. Botolph's Station or Osborne Street
2	5 4 4 3 2	Bus Station (Queen Street)
2	5 4 4 3 2 2	Holly Trees Museum
1	5 4 4 3 2 – –	Vineyard Street
1	6 5 4 4 3 3 2 2	Butt Rd. (Headgate) or Head St. or High St.
2	6 6 5 5 4 4 3 2 2	Wickham Road
3	7 6 6 5 4 4 4 3 3 2	Drury Hotel
4	8 7 6 6 5 5 5 4 4 3 2	Rainsborowe Road
5	9 8 7 7 6 6 5 5 5 4 3 2	Anzio Crescent
6	9 9 8 8 7 7 6 5 5 4 4 3 2	John Kent Avenue
7	10 9 9 8 7 7 7 6 6 5 5 4 3 2	Hedge Drive or Homefield Road
8	11 10 10 10 9 9 8 8 8 7 6 5 4 4 3	Berechurch Camp

High Street fares applicable to St. John's Green School.

Service 5 LEXDEN (Dugard Avenue)—BERGHOLT ROAD (Bakers Lane)
Service 5A LEXDEN (Borough Boundary)—TURNER ROAD (Mill Road)

FROM LEXDEN TO BERGHOLT ROAD or TURNER ROAD

Stage No.		
11		Dugard Avenue
10	2	Clairmont Road
10	– –	Borough Boundary
9	3 2 2	Halstead Road
8	4 3 3 2	Lexden Church
7	5 4 4 3 2	Fitzwalter Road
6	6 5 4 4 3 2	Park Road
5	6 5 5 5 4 3 2	Hospital
1	7 6 6 6 5 4 3 2	Head Street
2	8 7 7 6 5 4 4 3 2	Middleborough
3	8 7 7 7 6 5 4 3 2 2	Colne Bank Avenue
4	9 8 8 7 6 5 5 4 3 2 2	North Station
5	10 9 9 8 7 6 6 5 4 3 3 2	Mile End Footpath or Institution
6	10 10 10 9 8 7 7 6 5 4 4 3 2	Bakers Lane or Kingswood Road
7	11 10 10 9 9 8 7 6 6 5 4 3 2 2	Mill Road

Head Street fares applicable to St. Helena School.
Fitzwalter Road fares applicable to Norman Way (Girls' High School)

FROM BERGHOLT ROAD or TURNER ROAD TO LEXDEN

Stage No.		
7		Mill Road
6	2	Bakers Lane or Kingswood Road
5	2 2	Mile End Footpath or Institution
4	3 3 2	North Station
3	4 4 3 2	Colne Bank Avenue
2	5 4 3 2 2	Middleborough
1	6 5 4 3 2 2	High Street
2	6 6 5 4 3 2 2	Holly Trees Museum
3	6 6 5 4 4 3 3 2	Bus Station (Queen Street)
3	6 6 5 4 4 3 3 2 2	Osborne Street
4	6 6 5 4 4 3 3 3 2 2	Vineyard Street
5	6 6 5 4 4 3 3 3 3 3 2	Hospital
6	7 7 6 5 4 4 3 3 3 3 3 2	Park Road
7	8 7 6 5 5 4 4 4 4 4 4 3 2	Fitzwalter Road
8	9 8 7 6 6 5 5 5 5 5 5 4 3 2	Lexden Church
9	9 9 8 7 7 6 6 6 6 6 6 5 4 3 2	Halstead Road
10	10 10 9 8 7 7 6 6 6 6 6 5 4 4 3 2	Borough Boundary
10	10 10 9 8 7 7 6 6 6 6 6 5 5 4 3 2 –	Clairmont Road
11	11 10 10 9 8 8 7 7 7 7 7 6 6 5 4 3 – 2	Dugard Avenue

High Street fares applicable to St. Helena School.
Fitzwalter Road fares applicable to Norman Way (Girls' High School).

Service 6 OLD HEATH—SHRUB END ESTATE or PRETTYGATE

Stage No.		
9		Old Heath (Speedwell Road)
8	2	Abbots Road
7	3 2	Old Heath Post Office
6	3 2 2	Barnhall Avenue Jct. or Scarletts Road
5	4 3 3 2	Recreation Ground
4	5 4 3 3 2	Camp Church
3	5 5 4 4 3 2	St. Botolph's Station
3	5 5 4 4 3 2 –	Osborne Street
2	6 5 5 4 3 3 2 –	Bus Station (Queen Street)
2	6 5 5 4 3 3 2 – 2	Holly Trees Museum
2	6 5 5 4 3 3 – 2 – –	Vineyard Street
1	7 6 5 5 4 4 3 3 3 2 2	Head St. or High St.
2	7 7 6 6 5 4 4 3 4 3 2 2	Creffield Road
3	8 7 7 7 6 5 4 4 4 4 3 3 2	Cambridge Road
4	9 8 7 7 6 6 5 4 5 4 4 4 3 2	Drury Road
5	10 9 8 8 7 7 6 5 6 5 5 5 4 3 2	Walnut Tree Way
6	10 9 9 9 8 7 6 6 6 6 5 5 4 3 3 2	Willett Rd. or Hastings Rd.
7	11 10 10 9 8 8 7 7 7 7 6 6 5 4 3 2 2	Owen Ward Close or Prettygate S.C.
8	11 10 10 10 9 8 7 7 7 7 6 6 5 4 4 3 2 2	Hills Crescent West

Creffield Road fares are applicable to journeys between Old Heath Post Office and St. Helena School.
St. Botolph's Station fares are applicable to journeys between Hills Crescent West and St. Helena School.

Service 7 & 7A MERSEA ROAD or MONKWICK ESTATE—NORTH STATION

Stage No.		
11		Cherry Tree or Gosfield Road
10	2	Berechurch Hall Road or Bardfield Road
9	3 2	St. Margaret's Church or Sheering Walk
8	4 3 2	Normandy Avenue
7	5 4 3 2	Cemetery
6	5 4 3 2 2	Pownall Crescent
5	6 5 4 3 2 2	Napier Road
4	7 6 5 4 3 3 2	St. Botolph's Stn. or Osborne St.
3	7 6 5 4 4 3 3 2	Bus Station (Queen Street)
2	7 6 5 4 4 3 3 2 2	Holly Trees Museum
2	7 6 5 4 4 3 3 2 – –	Vineyard Street
1	8 7 6 5 4 4 3 3 3 2 2	Head St. or High St.
2	8 7 6 5 5 4 4 3 3 2 2 2	Middleborough
3	9 8 7 6 5 5 4 4 4 3 3 2 2	Colne Bank Ave.
4	9 8 7 6 6 6 5 4 4 4 4 3 2 2	North Station

Colne Bank Avenue fares applicable to Technical College (Sheepen Rd)

School Service HOMEFIELD ROAD—BERECHURCH SCHOOL

Stage No.		
7		Homefield Road
6	2	John Kent Avenue
5	3 2	Anzio Crescent
4	4 3 2	Rainsborowe Road
3	5 4 3 2	Drury Hotel
2	6 5 5 4 3	Berechurch School

LEXDEN—SHRUB END—HYTHE (Through Journeys Only)

Stage No.		
9		Lexden (Halstead Road)
8	2	Clairmont Road
7	3 2	Dugard Avenue
6	5 4 2	Leather Bottle
5	6 5 3 2	Walnut Tree Way
4	7 6 4 3 2	Drury Road
3	8 7 5 4 3 2	Cambridge Road
2	9 8 6 5 4 3 2	Creffield Road
1	10 9 7 6 5 4 3 2	Head Street or High Street
1	10 9 7 6 5 4 3 2 –	Vineyard Street
2	10 9 7 6 5 4 4 3 2 –	Holly Trees Museum
2	10 9 7 6 6 5 4 4 3 – 2	Bus Stn. (Queen St.)
3	10 9 7 6 5 4 4 3 – 2 – –	Osborne Street
3	10 10 9 8 6 5 4 4 3 – 2 2 –	St. Botolph's Station
4	11 11 10 9 8 7 6 6 4 3 3 3 2 2	Wimpole Rd
5	11 11 11 10 9 8 7 6 4 4 4 4 3 3 2	Port Lane
6	1/- 1/- 11 10 9 8 7 7 5 4 4 4 3 3 2 2	Hythe Quay or Paxmans (Port Lane)
7	1/1 1/1 1/- 11 10 9 8 8 6 5 5 5 4 4 3 3 2	Hawkins Rd. (Southern End)

GENERAL REGULATIONS

The Corporation will endeavour to ensure the correct operation of the services. but cannot be held responsible for any irregularities which may occur.

Passengers are warned not to board or alight whilst the 'bus is in motion.

It is an offence not to pay the conductor the fare appropriate to the journey taken, or to attempt to leave the 'bus without paying the fare, and with intent to avoid paying it.

Action will not normally be taken against any passenger who, being unable to pay for the journey taken, gives his or her name and address to the conductor and forwards the unpaid fare **direct to the General Manager, Corporation Transport, Magdalen Street, Colchester,** within 48 hours. A ticket will be issued by the conductor for the amount due.

Discount Tickets are obtainable from Transport Offices, Magdalen Street and Borough Treasurer's Dept., 64 West Stockwell Street in books of 12; 5d. tickets: 4/4½, 6d. tickets: 5/–. These are valid at all times except Sundays and Bank Holidays.

Children under three years of age carried free.

Children over three and under fourteen years of age are charged half the adult fare (minimum 1d.).

Children up to the age of 16 travelling to or from school are allowed to travel at half the adult fare (minimum 1d.).

Dogs are carried, at owner's risk and responsibility, in either the upper or the lower deck. They must be on a leash throughout the journey and must not occupy any seat or part of a seat. The charge for each dog shall be the same as the fare payable by the passenger in charge of the dog. When a dog accompanies an adult and a child the adult will be deemed to be in charge.

No other animals may be carried.

Luggage. Passengers are entitled to carry by hand on the 'buses personal luggage not of a bulky nature up to 28 lb. in weight. All other luggage not exceeding 56 lb., to be charged for at the rate of 1d. per package between Town Centre and any terminus. Luggage or parcels containing anything of an inflammable, dangerous or objectionable character are prohibited on the vehicle at any time.

Lost Property. In compliance with the P.S.V. (Lost Property) (Amendment) Regulations No. 2262/58, any article lost on a 'bus can be claimed at the Lost Property Office, Magdalen Street, Colchester, between the hours of 8.45 a.m. and 5.30 p.m. on Mondays to Fridays (except Bank Holidays). A booking fee of 6d. is charged, together with one-twelfth (maximum £4) of the value of the article which shall be awarded to the conductor. Postal enquiries should be accompanied by a stamped, addressed envelope.

IMPORTANT. The conditions and tables in this publication are liable to alteration at short notice.

J. GRAY,
General Manager.

Transport Offices,
Magdalen Street,
Colchester.
'Phone: 5101, *ext.* 3

22nd March, 1963

Essex Telegraph Press Ltd., Colchester

One Way Prelude

A small one-way traffic system was introduced on 4 June 1962 when all inward buses along Maldon Road were diverted via Wellesley Road which became one-way northbound while the northern end of Maldon Road became one-way southbound. This was just a taste of what was to follow in the next year.

From 29 July 1962 a short extension to the route of Prettygate journeys on services 1A and 6 along The Commons to the junction with Hills Crescent (West) was introduced and from the next day an all day service to Prettygate was provided on service 6. At the other end of the route, the duplication to and from Old Heath Post Office was re-routed via Barnhall Avenue to terminate in Barnhall Estate at Meopham Court, these journeys being officially numbered 6A (the Old Heath Post Office journeys had always shown number 6A but the route number never appeared in publicity until then).

A revised timetable for services 2/2A was introduced on 27 August 1962 which provided for a regular two-hourly extension of Mill Road journeys to and from Myland Hospital as well as some additional journeys for visiting hours.

New Bus Station

In 1961 the Council had opened a new Bus Station in Lewis's Gardens off East Hill and Queen Street for the country buses and express coach services. All these services were transferred from the old Bus Park in St Johns Street on 26 February 1961.

A proposal by the Council's Road Traffic Committee in July 1962 was considered by the Transport Committee that all the Corporation buses should divert through the Bus Station and observe bus stops on the Queen Street exit road which would relieve the traffic congestion caused by buses observing the stop at the top of Queen Street. It was decided to take no action on the rerouting but the offending bus stop was withdrawn from 19 November. However events in 1963 changed this decision.

Severe Problems

Mention should be made of the adverse weather conditions of the winter of 1962/63 which affected operations from December through to March. Probably the worst two days were 6 and 7 December when 18 buses were involved in accidents as a result of icy roads and dense fog. Six buses received severe damage to front or rear ends, one had both. The garage staff worked many hours to effect repairs and only a few peak hour journeys were lost on the following days.

One Way Introduced

Traffic congestion in Colchester in the early sixties was a problem which often delayed buses sometimes by more than half-an-hour. It was not uncommon on Saturday mornings for crews to be switched "across the road" in the High Street in order to put buses back on time! After much deliberation the Council decided to introduce an experimental one-way traffic system involving a clockwise circuit of High Street, Queen Street, St Botolphs Street, Osborne Street, Stanwell Street, St Johns Street and Head Street with a supplementary scheme at St Botolphs. In addition all buses were re-routed via the Bus Station with stops for Corporation buses in the Queen Street exit road, and stops in Vineyard Street (off Stanwell Street) for all westbound buses. The experiment started on 1 April 1963 and was considered to be a success despite some difficulties encountered by bus operators.

From the same date the frequency of service 1/1A was increased from every 15 minutes to every 10 minutes to cater for the expanding housing developments in the Greenstead and Shrub End areas. The route in Greenstead was extended from Sycamore Avenue along Hawthorn Avenue to Almond Way. Services 3 and 6A were also linked to provide a regular hourly cross-town service between Barnhall and St Andrews Avenue. As a result the fleet strength increased to 42 buses.

The Shrub End terminal of service 6 was adjusted from Owen Ward Close to Egerton Green Road from 9 March 1964 due to problems with parked cars in the narrow road.

Sixty Years On

The undertaking celebrated its Diamond Jubilee in 1964. Bus 22 (194MNO) was painted in a special livery and suitably decorated for operation on each route between 3 and 11 October. An exhibition was held in the Castle Museum and a booklet published

Wider Buses

The first eight foot wide buses were introduced in 1966 but the arrival of Leyland Atlantean demonstration vehicle KTD 551C had considerable impact when it operated on the town's bus services for ten days in August and September 1966, so much so that an order for three Leyland Titan PD2s was changed to Atlanteans, but still with Massey bodies. These were delivered in December 1967 followed by a further seven in 1968.

1916 Miss Ann Cudden, tram conductress in full uniform comprising heavy coat, full length skirt, and wide brim soft hat. Equipment includes ticket rack, bell punch, clippers all hung on substantial leather straps. The motorman (driver) stands on the platform.

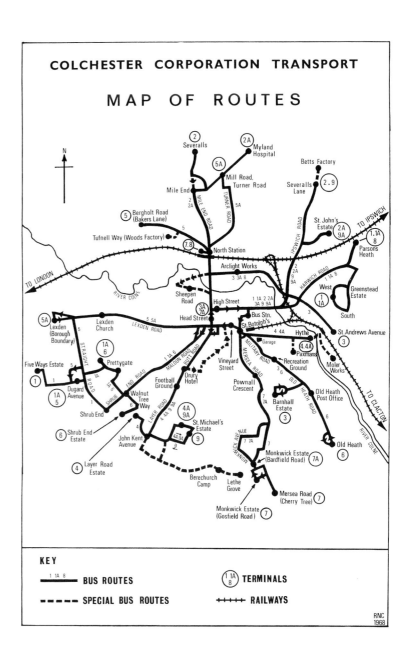

Map of Routes included in Timetable booklet 23 March 1969

With the advent of buses offering better weather protection the uniform was updated. An example of pre-1969 issue to drivers; note the white right hand cuff as an aid to hand signals.

Inspector's Office in number 2 Garage pre-1962 with Fred Tierney (right) and Jack Andrews guarding the doorway. Note the discreetly clad female on the calendar in direct contrast to those adorning the garage in the 90's.

Commuter Link

The improved rail service to and from London was making Colchester more attractive for commuters and as a result new service 8 was introduced with effect from 27 June 1966 to provide a more direct link between Parsons Heath and North Station. With two journeys each way on Mondays to Fridays, the service proved to be quite popular.

Beyond the Boundary

Development in Stanway, then outside the Borough saw the extension of some journeys on service 1 from Dugard Avenue to Fiveways Estate from 4 December 1966 and certain other journeys were diverted via Prettygate and Ambrose Avenue (service 1A) to give Prettygate a 15 minute frequency combined with service 6. On the other side of town expansion at Greenstead was catered for by an extension of service 1/1A to Elm Crescent from 3 September 1967 and the new St Johns Estate was served by a diversion of alternate journeys off Ipswich Road along Upland Drive to the shopping centre (service 2A) with effect from 22 October 1967.

The Homefield Road journeys on service 4, which had been cut back from Berechurch Camp, were diverted into the new military estate along Lordswood Road and Fallowfield Road to St Michael's (Alamein Road) from 8 January 1968 and were numbered 4A. From 8 July these journeys were re-routed towards Alamein Road via Baronswood Way, Peerswood Road and Earlswood Way to form an anti-clockwise loop.

Housing Estates Served

In 1969, services were again revised to cater for the expanding developments at Greenstead, St John's and St Michael's. From 23 March the 10 minute frequency on services 1 and 1A was altered to provide a half-hourly frequency on each of the three "legs" - to Parsons Heath, to Greenstead via the existing route and to Greenstead (Elm Crescent) via Hickory Avenue (north). Revised timetables were introduced on services 2/2A and 4/4A to co-ordinate with new half-hourly service 9/9A between Ipswich Road or St Johns and St Michael's. At Lexden, the Dugard Avenue journeys on service 5 were re-routed via Oaklands Avenue into Dugard Avenue to obviate reversing despite strong opposition from residents and at Monkwick, outward journeys on service 7 were re-routed via Berechurch Hall Road, Blackheath and Gosfield Road to the Wethersfield Road terminus with a view to future one-man-operation.

Staffing Problems

After protracted negotiations a limited amount of one-man operation on evenings and Sundays, using the Atlanteans, was introduced from 23 November 1969 on services 2, 5, 5A, 6 and 7. A serious shortage of staff also led to a reduction in frequencies during the evenings and on Sundays. This shortage was further aggravated by an outbreak of influenza and agreement was reached with the Traffic Commissioner and the Trade Unions to operate buses without conductors thus utilising drivers for whom no conductors could be found. Five of the Atlanteans were fitted with large honesty boxes on the cab door in which passengers could place their fares - no tickets were issued. A board was displayed on the bus "THIS IS A TRUST THE PASSENGER EMERGENCY SERVICE - NO CONDUCTOR ON THIS BUS". The arrangement started on 22 December and continued until the end of January.

Further Beyond The Borough

The construction of the Stanway by-pass (A12) together with road closures and diversions resulted in the removal of the King Coel Road terminus of service 5A at Lexden and from 9 March 1970 these buses were re-routed direct along London Road to Beacon End, Lucy Lane. Eastern National fares were charged beyond the Borough Boundary in what had previously been their territory.

The commuter service 8 between Parsons Heath and North Station was renumbered 11 from 20 July 1970 in anticipation of a major service revision. One-man operation of Service 3 commenced on 3 August initially using an Atlantean but subsequently with an AEC Reliance bus acquired from Hedingham & District. This marked a change in policy as it was the first second-hand vehicle and reintroduced single-deckers. Also on 3 August a revised timetable was introduced by G W Osborne & Sons on their Great Wigborough - Layer-de-la-Haye - Colchester service with a diversion via St Michael's and Gurdon Road, and CCT introduced some short journeys, numbered 10 to supplement the service between Kingsford Cross Roads and the town centre.

Buttons & Badges

LEYLAND PD2/MASSEY "MIDLAND RED" STYLE FRONTS

Above: 27: 9670 VX, in original livery after four years service is seen (left) in Ipswich Road at the Goring Road bus shelter, the undeveloped land in the background later becoming the Broadlands estate. Smartly attired in a new livery, 27 is seen (right) reversing at Hills Crescent, the Prettygate terminus of route 6, during February 1966.

LEYLAND PD2/MASSEY "St HELENS" STYLE FRONTS

Centre left: 35: MWC135 caught at work on the second day in service at the Recreation Hotel tram terminus (1906-1929) on the 2nd March 1963. Centre right: 37: CWC37B was barely three weeks old when the annual carnival parade took place in July 1964. The opportunity was taken to publicise the Diamond Jubilee of the municipal enterprise as shown at the Cavalry Barracks parade ground. Bottom left: 42: OVX142D celebrates the first regular stage working outside the borough boundary, seen turning into Winstree Road on Sunday 4 December 1966, departing Fiveways estate on the first journey. Bottom right: 41: OVX141D, seen October 1971 passing Dilbridge Road on Harwich Road. This bus had a livery variation from new with no upper deck red band and no fleetname on the lower deck band. More significantly, platform doors have been fitted, a welcome feature. G.R.Mills(6)

REAR ENGINED DOUBLE DECKERS ... THE FIRST TEN

Top left: 46: WEV746F is seen when brand-new in December 1967 reversing into Oaklands Avenue. The conductor has already set the side blind to Parsons Heath for the next journey. Top right: Repainted into blue and yellow, 46 was retained for eight years as a driver training vehicle as shown at work in September 1983 passing along London Road in Lexden. Centre left: 48: YWC648F, sporting a livery variation that was not perpetuated with two false bands to simplify repainting, is seen turning from the bus station into Queen Street in May 1973. Centre right: 49: YWC649F, seen in the bus station during August 1982 (when the multi-storey car park was still in situ) displays a much more attractive livery variation.

OPEN TOP IN TOWN FLEET AFTER NEARLY 50 YEARS

Below left: 48 was to outlive the entire batch by virtue of roof removal in 1979. In 1984 lettering was added to mark 80 years of CBT and the fleetname Colchester Corporation Tramways was applied as shown in this July shot as the bus turns into Cowdray Crescent (War Memorial/Castle Gates) from the High Street for the seasonal 2pm departure. Below right: 48 received the final livery design as applied to later Atlanteans and Olympians and is seen outside the CBT offices then in Osborne Street (ex Eastern Electricity) with 53 (MVK 548R) one of the three ex Tyne & Wear AN68/Alexander at the rear. After CBT service, 48 went on to work for Blue Bus at Felixstowe, Bulleys Bus at Paignton/Torquay and, even further, to Maghull Coaches, Bootle, to operate a Liverpool city tour.   G R Mills (6)

Left to right: CBT Coachways red lines on blue background; CBT standard; Formation of limited company in 1986 issue; final CBT style blue lines on a maroon background.

TIM machine specially sprayed in gold and presented to Tom Stafford on his retirement as chief inspector. Use by his grandchildren has worn much of the paintwork!

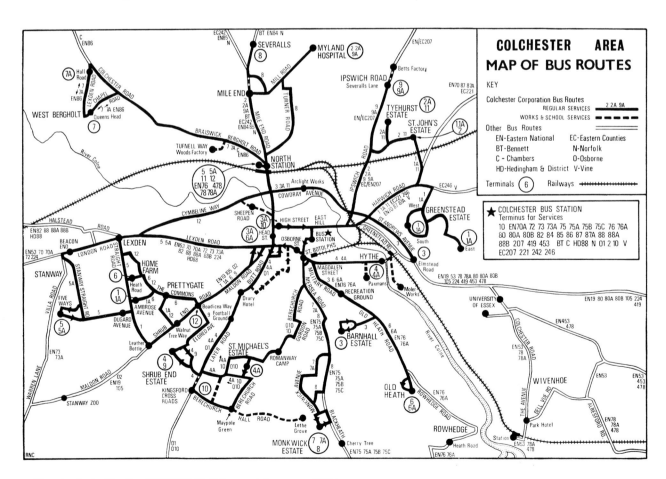

Map included in the TIMETABLE issued January 1971

Major Service Upheaval

One of the most extensive revisions to services took place on 24 January 1971 affecting all timetables and many routes, the more notable aspects being the extension of services in Stanway and the replacement of Eastern National buses to and from West Bergholt. The new and revised services were as follows:

Service	Route	Basic weekday frequency
1/1A	Greenstead Estate or St John's Estate - Harwich Road - Town Centre - Shrub End or Prettygate - Ambrose Avenue	10 minutes
2/2A	St John's Estate or Tyehurst - Ipswich Road - Town Centre - North Station - Mile End - Mill Road - Myland Hospital	15 minutes
3/3A	Barnhall Estate - Town Centre - Cowdray Avenue - St Andrews Avenue	60 minutes
4/4A	Hythe - Town Centre - Layer Road - Shrub End Estate or St Michael's Estate	15 minutes
5/5A	Stanway, Five Ways - Dugard Avenue or Beacon End – Lexden - Town Centre - North Station	15 minutes
6/6A	Old Heath - Town Centre - Prettygate - Home Farm	15 minutes
7/7A	Monkwick - Town Centre - North Station - West Bergholt	30 minutes
8	Monkwick - Town Centre - North Station - Turner Road – Severalls	30 minutes
9	Ipswich Road - Town Centre - Maldon Road - Shrub End Estate	30 minutes
9A	Ipswich Road - Town Centre - North Station - Mile End - Myland Hospital Early mornings, evenings and Sundays only	
10	Kingsford Cross Road - St Michael's - Gurdon Road - Town centre	occasional journeys
11	Tyehurst - St John's - Cowdray Avenue - North Station	Monday – Friday commuter service
12	Shrub End - Prettygate - Home Farm - Lexden - North Station	Monday – Friday commuter service

The revision involved the introduction of one-man operation all day on 6/6A, using the Atlanteans, as well as on most of the peak hour duplication, works and school buses and services 10, 11 and 12. This required the hire of four AEC Reliances from Great Yarmouth Corporation Transport, one of which was retained until July. In February six former Salford City Transport AEC Reliances were acquired from SELNEC PTE, and for a time operated in Salford's distinctive dark green livery before being repainted. These were joined by another five AEC Reliances from Leicester City Transport in November for more one-man operation.

Sunday Treats

Further adventures into Stanway came with the operation of two summer Sunday afternoon services to Colchester Zoo from Greenstead, North Station, Lexden and Old Heath, Barnhall, Monkwick, St Michael's and Shrub End starting on 16 May 1971.

Revised evening timetables were introduced from 21 June 1971 on all services except 1/1A which resulted in some routes having less frequent and irregular timetables. This was followed by a general reduction of Sunday services from 21 November. From the same date services 5/5A were converted to all day one man operation with Atlanteans and the former Leicester Reliances.

Christmas Park and Ride

A Park and Ride service was operated from December 6 to Christmas Eve (Mondays to Saturdays) between Cavalry Barracks and the Town Centre every 5-10 minutes, between 0915 and 1730 hours. Four single deck buses (Bristol LS's) were hired from and operated by Eastern National under the banner "Lancer Buslink". The operation was considered to be a success and was continued after Christmas on Saturdays using the Salford Reliances, but demand was low and the service ceased after 5 February 1972.

The summer Sunday services to Colchester Zoo were revised for the 1972 season but combined into one service with two return journeys. The route linked Ipswich Road (Severalls Lane), St Johns, Bridgebrook, Greenstead, Hythe, Old Heath, Barnhall, Monkwick, St Michael's, Shrub End, Prettygate and Five Ways to Stanway Zoo from Easter but a Mondays to Saturdays hourly service over this route between Ipswich Road and Five Ways commenced on 28 May and was numbered 12 - the existing service 12 (Shrub End - North Station) being numbered 12A. From the same date services 4/4A were extended beyond Hythe into Greenstead estate which resulted in the frequency of services 1/1A being reduced to every 15 minutes. There were also alterations to services 2/2A, 6/6A and 9/9A. Some additional Monday to Friday peak period journeys were introduced on service 1A between Bridgebrook and Town Centre from 10 July.

UNIQUE 55 THE 2ND

55: 652GVA, a 1963 AEC Reliance 470 with attractive Plaxton Highway body achieved several firsts. The bus was the first second-hand vehicle, the first pay on entry bus and the first post-war single-decker with Colchester Corporation Transport and is seen at work in St Andrews Avenue during September 1970. New to Irvine (Golden Eagle), based in Salsburgh, Lanarkshire, 55 came from Hedingham Omnibuses and was used in the borough for nearly five years before sale via Ensign to the well known Bebb, Llantwit Fadre in South Wales.

SECOND-HAND SINGLE-DECKERS

Centre Left: 1: TRJ109 was one of six ex Salford AEC Reliance 470s with Weymann bodies purchased to introduce additional pay on entry o-m-o workings. Only four of the six were repainted in Colchester livery; as shown at work in St Andrews Avenue during May 1973. Centre Right: 3: TRJ103, one of the pair that remained in as acquired green livery with Colchester Corporation fleetname on the waistband, is seen at the North Rail Station in April 1971.

Right: 10: ABC196B was one of five AEC Reliance 470s with Marshall bodies that were initially new to Leicester as B54F but were later converted to B50D for park and ride duties. Prior to arrival in Colchester all five were converted to B53F by Willowbrook of Loughborough. When seen in Holly Road, Stanway during December 1971, 10 clearly illustrates that all evidence of the centre exit, which was sited immediately ahead of the rear axle, has been expertly removed. All the second-hand AEC Reliances (except 2 and 3 which went for scrap) were sold for further service by Ensign. G.R.Mills(4)

Cancelled Double Deckers

An order for three more Atlanteans was cancelled in 1971 but an order for fifteen ECW bodied Bristol RE's was placed, the first five of which were delivered in May 1972 enabling a further increase in one-man operation.

The Saturday timetable on the new service 12 was withdrawn after 25 November because of very low ridership but some Saturday morning journeys on service 1A between Bridgebrook and Town Centre commenced on 2 December 1972. The Park and Ride service between Cavalry Barracks and Town Centre was reintroduced for the four Saturdays before Christmas, this time using three Bristol RE's and was numbered X72.

Town's First Bus Lane

The opening of the southern section of the town's inner relief road, Southway, on 3 March 1973 saw the introduction of a contra-flow bus lane at the northern end of Maldon Road and a bus only facility from St John's Street into Crouch Street at Headgate as part of a general revision to traffic flows in that part of the town centre.

Further changes to services in the eastern area of the town were made from 6 May 1973. All the daytime journeys on services 1/1A operated into Greenstead Estate whilst the St John's and Bridgebrook journeys were covered by a revised service 9 between Ipswich Road and Shrub End Estate via St John's and Harwich Road. Service 2 was extended to Magdalen Wood and service 2A diverted off Ipswich Road also to Magdalen Wood to interwork. The service linking the estates in the east, south and west of town (12) suffered a further reduction with a reduced off-peak service of every 90 minutes running between Monkwick and Ipswich Road but a new facility to the University of Essex was introduced with a double run from Elmstead Road roundabout these journeys being numbered 12A, whilst the Shrub End - North Station journeys reverted to being numbered 12. However this was not a success and the timetable was further reduced to a small number of peak journeys from 24 December.

OMO Hires

The second and third batches of five Bristol RE's were delivered in May and December 1973 but in order to facilitate one man operation of services 1/1A from 2 September vehicles were hired from Hedingham & District, Great Yarmouth Transport and Southend Transport. The Park & Ride service was again operated on the four Saturdays before Christmas and this year it was numbered X73.

Opposition

An application in June 1973 to operate part of services 2/2A to Horkesley Heath was met by objection from W. Norfolk & Sons and the matter lay unresolved for much of 1974 but following meetings with Essex County Council's Transport Co-ordination Officers the application was eventually withdrawn.

The reorganisation of local government in 1974 resulted in the transport undertaking being renamed Colchester Borough Transport from 1 April.

New Admin Centre

The offices at Magdalen Street were becoming very cramped and the employees' facilities were very poor so opportunity was taken to move into the former Eastern Electricity Board offices in Osborne Street in June 1974. Drivers and conductors started and finished their duties at Osborne Street and, although it was still necessary to collect or return a bus to the Magdalen Street garage, all changeovers could be made at the bus stops outside the offices with good supervision. The move enabled much needed changes to take place at Magdalen Street for the engineering staff.

The Park & Ride service for Christmas shoppers ran on the three Saturdays before Christmas in 1974, but only every ten minutes using a Ford demonstrator and one of the AEC Reliances. The service was numbered X25.

Double Deckers regain Favour

April 1975 saw a further change of vehicle policy with a reversion to double-deck buses with the delivery of six Leyland Atlantean AN68s with ECW bodywork; these had the distinctive "Sheffield style" peaked roof. They were to be followed by a further thirty such buses between 1976 and 1980 although the ECW bodywork was of the traditional "rounded-domes" style.

Service 9 (Ipswich Road - Shrub End Estate) was re-routed via Goring Road and Ipswich Road between Harwich Road and East Street from 1 April 1975.

NEW CHASSIS MAKE THREE BATCHES THREE LIVERIES

25: SWC25K one of the first batch of five Bristol RELL/ECW is seen in Osborne Street, with St Botolph's Church tower in the background when brand new (note the bright wheel nuts) about to take up service 6A in May 1972. Within easy walking distance of the depot the Osborne Street stands are regularly used for driver shift changes.

15: YWC15L one of second batch of five, was delivered in 1973 in the same livery as 25 (above). For a special display in the Castle Park in August 1974 a different paintwork style and colour was applied – a central band was added in a non-standard rosy red which was also used around the front grille, which gave a "lipstick" mouth look to the bus. On repaint, 15 received the final RE style as on 23 (below).

14-28

23: OWC723M was one of the third batch of five, which again were all delivered in the same livery as 25 (top) but by final repaint had received the enhanced red band and roof styling. Since 1960 each type of borough bus has been the subject of a farewell tour organised by the PSV Circle's Colchester meeting. This was the case in May 1988 when 23 visited Norfolks at Nayland (owners of three ex West Yorkshire examples) as seen in Parkers Way, Nayland. 23 was one of 7 (out of the 15 REs) which passed to Busways, Newcastle-upon-Tyne. GR Mills (3)

SPECIAL 55 THE THIRD

Top left: 55: JHK495N One of six of the AN68 type Atlanteans with many improved mechanical features; fitted with the rare 'Sheffield style' ECW body. 55 certainly continued to Colchester tradition of being a special when allocated the 'special' fleet number. Original livery style but the cream replaced by silver celebrating the Queen's Jubilee in 1977 as seen at Lexden Church January 1978 with 64: NNO64P at work on school specials.

GR Mills (6)

Top Right: 55 received a modified front panel and a livery variation with black lower deck window surrounds shown as the bus turns from East Hill into the bus station in July 1988. Centre Left: 57 (JHK 497N) is seen when brand new departing the Five Ways terminus at Stanway in April 1975. Centre Right: 60 (JHK 500N) is seen in Osborne Street during September 1987 with a curious frontal paint style. Note the extra glazed aperture in the front corner pillar, added to aid the driver's vision. Lower Left: 55 again! Seen when converted to open top in St John's Street during July 1993 proclaiming Colchester as "Camulodunum – Britain's oldest recorded town". Bottom Right: The oldest CBT bus to receive Arriva livery albeit after 55 (as 5301) had ceased operation of the town tour in September 2000. Seen at the Southend Transport depot in Short Street, sporting a diagrammatic map of the Shires & Essex operations.

Park & Ride Experiment

A new Park & Ride service was introduced on 13 December 1975 between the British Rail overflow car park at North Station and the Town Centre on Saturdays for a six month experiment with grant-aid from Essex County Council. However it ceased after 6 March 1976 due to poor patronage.

In order to provide another facility into the Greenstead Estate, service 3 was extended beyond St Andrews Avenue to Hamlet Drive and linked to a new service 3A via Harwich Road, Goring Road, Ipswich Road and East Hill to and from the Town Centre with effect from 7 February 1977. Consequently service 9 was re-routed via Harwich Road, St Andrews Avenue and Ipswich Road. Also, the two journeys which terminated at Tyehurst on service 2 and the commuter service 11 were extended via St Cyrus Road to Magdalen Wood.

A short but controversial bus lane was introduced at Middleborough in April 1977 which effectively precluded all traffic except buses proceeding up North Hill towards town. After only a few months, it was removed following protests from businesses on North Hill.

The Summer Sunday journeys to Stanway Zoo on service 12 were not reintroduced at Easter 1978 but instead a Wednesday afternoon service was operated during the summer school holidays and numbered 12A.

Bus Station Reorientated

A reorganisation of the Bus Station took place on 29 October 1978 in which the flow between the bus stands was reversed to run north to south. This permitted CBT to use stands 15 - 17 instead of temporary stops in the south-west corner of the Bus Station, referred to as "The Triangle".

Open Top Tours

As part of a "Tourism in Colchester Week" promotion in November 1978, circular tours were operated on 11th and 12th, and then introduced for the summer of 1979 from 27 May to 30 September on Sundays, Tuesdays, Wednesdays and Thursdays. Initially ordinary Atlanteans were used but one of the original batch, bus 48, was converted to open-top in August primarily for use on the tour. It is worth noting that this bus, after life in Colchester, also ran in Felixstowe, Torquay and Liverpool. Various other local tours were included on the licence but never operated.

Weather Problems

In 1979, heavy snow on Wednesday 14 February resulted in services being withdrawn during the evening and none were operated on Thursday 15. Because of poor road conditions and the reduced number of buses available it was necessary to run emergency timetables on Friday 16 and Saturday 17. The following weekend, two new Leyland Leopards with Duple bodywork were delivered (nos 101/102) which were suitable for both bus and coach work.

The 75th Anniversary of the undertaking was achieved in 1979 and bus 75 (TPU75R) was painted in a special livery to commemorate the event.

Another revision of evening and Sunday timetables was introduced on 4 November 1979 providing frequencies of a more regular nature to replace the somewhat untidy operation that had existed for some eight years. A new Sunday afternoon service between Ipswich Road and the Town Centre via Bridgebrook and Goring Road, numbered 9A , was also introduced. The journeys on service 12 between Lexden and North Station were renumbered 15.

The end of January 1980 saw the last of the Leyland Titan PD2s withdrawn from service without ceremony being replaced by Leyland AN68s.

Off Track

Rail replacement services for pre-determined and emergency work were now being provided, albeit as sub-contracted work through Eastern National. A major task taken on over the weekend of 23/24 February 1980 saw the combined forces of three local authority undertakings, Colchester, Ipswich and Southend, providing rail replacement services between Colchester, Ipswich and Harwich.

Joint Services Introduced

A revision to some Saturday services took place on 13 September 1980 which particularly affected early morning and late afternoon timetables to reflect the lower patronage at these times. More significant changes followed from 4 January 1981 in an effort to reduce operating costs. They were significant because the first joint service between Colchester Borough Transport and Eastern National was introduced on services 6 and 76 from the Town Centre to Old Heath and Rowhedge, utilising two Colchester buses and one from Eastern National. As a consequence, the section of service 6/6A between Town Centre and Home Farm was replaced by diverting part of service 9 to Home Farm and on to Lexden, these journeys were numbered 9A. The timetables of services 1, 1A, 9 and 9A were designed to provide a ten minute frequency along Harwich Road and Maldon Road. The service 3A between Greenstead and the Town Centre was withdrawn but a new Monday to Friday peak period service 13 was introduced running via Goring Road but with only one journey each way. Among other revisions, services 7/7A and 8 exchanged routes in Monkwick estate. Most evening and Sunday journeys were revised to operate on reduced running times and the Sunday afternoon service 9A was withdrawn.

UTILITY Top left: 39: JTW982 Guy Arab/Weymann at John Kent Avenue in April 1960 prepares to return to town. The conductor walks back to Catherine Hunt Way before blowing his whistle to indicate it is safe to reverse the bus around. Top right: 46: KEV331 Bristol K6A/Duple has already completed the manoeuvre the Guy is about to undertake, and waits in John Kent Avenue in August 1963 ready to make a return journey to Monkwick Estate.

POST WAR

52: KPU516 AEC Regent II/Massey. The strong pre-war traits of the body style can be seen in this view at the Welshwood Park Road terminus in Harwich Road, Parsons Heath during November 1965. This turn was abandoned in favour of serving Greenstead Estate and the bus was withdrawn 3 months later.

RR Eves

THE SPECIAL 55

55: KPU519 the unique Crossley/Massey could not be allowed to be withdrawn without ceremony. Accordingly on 24 September 1967 the bus was duly hired by the Colchester PSV Circle meeting to initially line-up with the four all Crossley deckers and then taken on tour to find fellow holders of fleet no. 55. Bottom left: Colchester 55 meets ex Great Yarmouth 55 EX5935 Leyland PD1/Massey at Mulleys Motorways yard at Acton, near Sudbury. Bottom right: Colchester 55 meets Ipswich 55: PPV55 AEC Regent V/East Lancs at Constantine Road depot by the rear of Ipswich Town FC ground. GR Mills (4)

Top left: 1:OHK429 Daimler CVD6/Roberts the only one of the batch to receive the experimental 'sandwich' livery. Seen in Layer Road during February 1966. GR Mills

Top right: 6:SVW451 all Crossley was also the only one of the set chosen to wear the 'sandwich' style paint scheme. Seen in September 1964 against a background of jumbled buildings all of which were demolished to make way for St Botolphs roundabout. RN Collins

Centre left: 11:WPU733 AEC Regent III/Massey one of the last trio of exposed radiator types. Seen opposite Lexden Church in Lexden Road during August 1963. RN Collins

Centre right: 21:193MNO AEC Regent V/Massey one of the final clutch of three, which brought the total operated to eleven. Seen in Mill Road, by Severalls staff houses in April 1965. RR Eves

LAST HALF CABS

Bottom left: 29:MWC129 Leyland PD2A/Massey the first of a batch of seven with 'St Helens' style fibreglass fronts. Seen in Hawthorn Avenue, Greenstead Estate in July 1967. RR Eves

Bottom Right: 39:OVX139D Leyland PD2A/Massey one of the last six front-engined, rear entrance deckers but the first 8 foot wide models. Fitted with platform doors in November 1970 in the livery adopted in 1966 and perpetuated through to the Atlantean/Massey era. Seen at St Johns Estate shopping parade in October 1967. RR Eves

Top left: 53:AVX53G the penultimate of ten Leyland Atlantean/Massey new 1967/8, attired in 'layer cake' layout livery. Seen in Osborne Street during August 1975.   RN Collins

Top right: 25:SWC25K one of the first batch of five Bristol RELL6L/ECW (two more sets of five followed). Seen in Circular Road West on a gloomy day in December 1972 at work on the Christmas Park & Ride service X72 from Cavalry Barracks.   RN Collins

Centre left: 55:JHK495N the first of the 'Sheffield' style ECW/Leyland Atlanteans converted to open-top for the seasonal town tours. Seen entered in the town's annual carnival procession in July 1994 with 84:MEV84V at rear in special 90 years service livery on Abbey Field.   GR Mills

Centre right: 102:PHK102T one of a pair of Leyland Leopard/Duple took CBT liveried stock well beyond the borough boundary. Seen in London Victoria on hire to National Express working 084 service during the rail strike in 1982.   RN Collins

COLCHESTER BOROUGH... LAST NEW DELIVERIES

Bottom left: 43:D43RWC all Leyland Olympian works the first day's journeys on the Saturdays only service 25 to Ipswich. Seen on 18th April 1987 at Manningtree level crossing returning home. Brantham village and the Stour river visible in background.   RR Eves

Bottom right: 27:K27EWC all Leyland Lynx, the last new bus ever supplied to CBT. Seen when brand new in September 1992 at Tollgate, Stanway.   GR Mills

Top left: 3308: NIW6508 (ex GUA821N) 1974 Leyland National rebuilt to Greenway style in 1993. Seen at work in Newcastle Avenue, Westlands during August 2000. Transferred to Harlow the following month.
Top right: 3315: A855UYM 1984 Volvo 810M with 1992 East Lancs body; out on a Sunday working for Great Eastern Railway operating from Witham via Chelmsford to Ingatestone during November 1999.

Left: 5369: BYX299V One of eight fully refurbished ex London Metrobuses injected into Colchester to replace the remaining Atlantean/ECW stock. Seen at Thomas Lord Audley School,in Monkwick about to work an Essex CC contract to Mersea Island during February 2002.

ARRIVA INTAKE GONE BY MID 2002

Bottom left: 5377: TPD107X the first of a trio of Leyland Olympians with distinctive Roe bodies as supplied to London Country. Seen at Shrub End sports ground during April 2001.
Bottom right: 3081: F153KGS Volvo B10M Plaxton Derwent II one of four which ousted Greenways; but these were not popular with elderly passengers on account of the high floor. Seen in Shrub End Road in September 2000. The bus was transferred away from Colchester within a year.   GR Mills (5)

Further Changes

October 1981 saw the rerouting of service 9A to operate as a loop around the Home Farm area and the withdrawal of service 13. The frequency of services 5 and 5A was reduced to every 20 minutes, made up of two 5A and one 5 journeys each hour.

The next major area of development in Colchester was at Highwoods, off Ipswich Road. From 2 November 1981, services 2 and 2A were extended beyond the Magdalen Wood terminus to Highwoods Square where a new shopping centre was to be built.

A school contract service provided by Essex County Council and operated by W Norfolk & Sons of Nayland between West Bergholt and Stanway Secondary School was withdrawn in April 1982. In replacement Colchester Borough Transport and Norfolks introduced a new joint service 17 from 19 April, each operator providing one bus.

After a period of three years with no new vehicles taken into stock, three second-hand buses were acquired in the autumn of 1983 from Tyne & Wear PTE. These were Leyland Atlantean AN68s with Alexander dual-door bodies and nearside staircases. The centre doors were removed before delivery.

Wider Reaching Co-ordination

During 1983, discussions commenced on a major rationalisation of bus services in Colchester involving Colchester Borough Transport, Eastern National and Hedingham Omnibuses under the guidance of Essex County Council's Transport Co-ordination Unit. These discussions resulted in several improvements being introduced from 6 May 1984:
a) More direct links to North Station
b) Easier access to the new General Hospital
c) Regular interval services along the main roads
d) Two area Travelcards for regular users
e) Wider availability of travel concessions for the elderly

The more significant changes to Colchester Borough Transport services included a revision of service 5/5A to run every 30 minutes, which, combined with Eastern National and Hedingham Omnibuses resulted in the provision of a bus every 10 minutes during the day along Lexden Road. Services 7/7A were revised to run between West Bergholt and West Mersea, omitting Monkwick, being jointly operated with Eastern National and incorporating their service 75 group. Each operator provided two buses. This new route was 14 miles long – the longest regular CBT bus route - and encountered a problem of flooding when high tides crossed The Strood, the road on to Mersea Island. Copies of the local tide tables were kept in the controllers office so that any necessary re-scheduling could be arranged for buses to be turned or replacement journeys provided on the mainland whilst buses were "stranded" on the island. Service 9/9A were altered to operate as circular routes from the yet to be opened General Hospital in Turner Road and serving Ipswich Road, Magdalen Wood, Bridgebrook, Harwich Road, town centre, Shrub End or Prettygate, Lexden and North Station, with the reverse direction numbered 19/19A. Colchester Borough Transport also started running to Wivenhoe via Essex University every hour on service 74A as part of a 15 minute frequency with Eastern National's 74 and 78/78A to Clacton and Brightlingsea. The already joint service 76 to Rowhedge was renumbered 6A. The changes became fully operational with the opening of the new General Hospital on 19 November 1984.

80th Milestone Passed

The undertaking celebrated its 80th Anniversary by running open top bus 48 on a special service on Saturday 28 July 1984 between North Station and Lexden following as closely as practicable one of the original tram routes.

The circular services 9/9A/19/19A were revised from 19 June 1985 with the General Hospital not being served on Saturdays, the services being curtailed to operate between Ipswich Road (Severalls Lane) via Town Centre to Lexden (Halstead Road corner) only on this day.

Air Suspension Luxury

A new generation of double-deck buses was introduced into the fleet in October 1985 with the delivery of two Leyland Olympians with ECW bodywork, followed by a further two in September 1986. The new generation of single-deck buses came with the all-Leyland Lynx, two of which were delivered in October 1986 after one (31) had been exhibited at the International Motor Show at Birmingham.

De-regulation Dawns

The Transport Act 1985 received Royal Assent on 30 October 1985 and set off the biggest changes in the operation of British bus services for over fifty years. Operators had to register services which they considered could be provided on a commercial basis by February 1986. After this date, County Council's would decide which other services should be provided on a contractual basis. Local authority bus undertakings, such as Colchester's, were to be transferred into limited companies owned by the Council but operated "at arms length" by a Board of Directors. Colchester Borough Transport Limited was thus formed ready for deregulation day (D-Day) on 26 October 1986. The Board of Directors consisted of three executive directors and three non-executive directors (one each representing the political parties nominated by the Borough Council).

Services from D-Day

The following commercial services commenced on D-Day on Mondays to Saturdays (no Sunday services were registered):

Service	Route
1/1A/1B	Greenstead or Longridge Park - Harwich Road - Town Centre - Maldon Road - Leather Bottle or Prettygate - Ambrose Avenue
2/2A/2B	Highwoods - St Johns - Ipswich Road - Town Centre - North Station - Mile End - Myland Hospital
3	Barnhall - Town Centre - North Station - Cowdray Avenue - St Andrews Avenue - Longridge Park
4/4A	Greenstead - Hythe - Town Centre - Layer Road - Shrub End or St Michaels
5/5A	Stanway, Five Ways - Dugard Avenue or Beacon End - Lexden - Town Centre - North Station - General Hospital - Myland Hospital
6/6A	Town Centre - Old Heath - Rowhedge
7/7A	West Bergholt - North Station - Town Centre - Blackheath - Abberton - Peldon - West Mersea
8	Severalls - General Hospital - North Station - Town Centre - Mersea Road - Monkwick
9/9A	General Hospital or Highwoods - St Johns - Bridgebrook - Harwich Road - Town Centre - Maldon Road - Shrub End or Prettygate - Lexden (Halstead Road Corner)
74A	North Station - Town Centre - Essex University - Wivenhoe

The following services were won on tender and operated under contract to Essex County Council:

10	St Michael's - Gurdon Road - Town Centre (Mondays to Fridays, two peak hour journeys)
11	Highwoods - Tyehurst - St Johns - Harwich Road - Cowdray Avenue - North Station (Mondays to Fridays commuter service)
13	Old Heath - Barnhall - Monkwick, Thomas Lord Audley School (Schooldays from 2 September 1986)
14	Monkwick - Barnhall - Hythe - Greenstead - St Johns - Ipswich Road (Mondays to Fridays works service)
14A	Ipswich Road- St Johns - Goring Road - Greenstead, Sir Charles Lucas School (Schooldays)
15	Shrub End - Prettygate - Lexden - North Station (Mondays to Fridays commuter service)
16	Old Heath - Sheepen Road, St Helena School (Schooldays from 2 September 1986)
75	Rowhedge - Fingringhoe - Abberton - Monkwick - Mersea Road - Town Centre (Mondays to Fridays, two peak hour journeys)
83	Wakes Colne - Great Tey - Marks Tey - Lexden - Town Centre (Mondays to Fridays, one peak journey)

Sabbath Day of Rest

Sunday services were provided in the town but these were operated by Eastern National under contract to Essex County Council, and so the doors to Magdalen Street garage were closed on Sundays for the time being.

The Colchester Travelcard scheme was also registered and continued to operate but these could not be used on buses operated under contract to Essex County Council. This caused considerable confusion to the travelling public, particularly as it was effectively not valid on Sundays.

The registered commercial services had to operate unaltered until 26 January 1987 when CBT took the opportunity to introduce various improvements:

The service 1B journeys to Longridge Park were re-routed to Greenstead East as service 1 and a new service 31 was introduced, running hourly from the General Hospital via North Station, Town Centre and Harwich Road to Longridge Park. As a consequence, service 3 was amended to interwork with the new 31. The service along Ipswich Road was improved on Mondays to Fridays daytime with the addition of half hourly service 2B between the Town Centre and Highwoods via Tyehurst, this combined with service 2/2A to give a ten minute frequency.

From 24 February 1987, service 5A was extended beyond Five Ways to the Tollgate shopping complex in Stanway to the new Sainsbury's store.

On the other side of town, as well as the normal bus services to and from Highwoods, where a large Tesco supermarket had opened, CBT also provided free bus services under contract to Tesco. These commenced in September 1986 and served Clacton, Dovercourt, Sudbury and later Wivenhoe on at least two days each week.

Wayfarer ticket

STANDARD'S AS HOARDINGS

The largest intake of standard buses in Colchester – 30 Leyland Atlantean AN68s with ECW 74 seat bodies were taken into stock from 1976 to 1980. Top left: 61: NNO61P is seen in bright yellow passing Greyfriars at the top of East Hill in April 1986. Top right: 82: YNO82S, in sombre blue, at the Hippodrome in the High Street during January 1985. The bus in the background is a Bristol RELL/ECW near the Town Hall. 82 was previously the pioneer overall advert bus (see back cover). Centre left: 84: MEV84V, in unrelieved red, turns out of the bus station into Queen Street in August 1983, passing the department store built for T M Locke, later Keddies and further principally Peacocks. The bridge over the road and the escalator, both in use in the background, were later demolished. Centre right: 86: MEV86V celebrates a century of municipal public transport in Britain passing the Bay & Say pub (previously The Lamb) in the High Street during July 1983. The white building in the background is now Angel Court. Bottom left: 86: MEV86V in base white and blue having been repainted for a second advertiser stops in High Street in January 1986. Claydons shop in the background had been The Angel pub, hence the naming of Angel Court at present on the site. Bottom right: 87: MEV87V, the second AN68 to receive an all-over advert was also the first for Broseley Homes, and is seen in Magdalen Street during June 1980 when only six months old. The building contractor sponsored many educational visits for schools which took the bus to a wide variety of destinations on private hire duties. The Waterloo Pub in the background was demolished to make way for a new building for the YMCA, Williamson House. GR Mills (6)

IN CELEBRATION

75: TPU75R Each major milestone has been marked with a special liveried bus – the half century with a Crossley; and 60 years with an AEC Regent V. For the ¾ century a very appropriately numbered bus was chosen to receive this predominantly cream paint scheme with bold "Starsky & Hutch" (from the American TV cop series) style stripe at the rear. 75 is seen in Layer Road bound for Paxman Avenue on Shrub End Estate during October 1979. The King's Ford Primary and Junior School playing fields are in the background.

90 YEARS SERVICE

84: MEV84V Unfortunately the obvious choice of bus 90 was upstaged by 84 which was in the paintshop at the time the decision to present a bus in pre-war livery was made. 84 is seen resplendent in the commemorative design with a very bold COLCHESTER CORPORATION fleetname, in Shrub End Road during July 1994 exactly 90 years from when the trams started. The destination should read Greenstead Estate as the bus has come from Ambrose Avenue. 90 achieved fame in a very well attended farewell to the breed in December 1999 (see back cover).

COACHES INTRODUCED

102: DHK102T was one of a pair of Leyland Leopards with Duple Dominant II bodies new in February 1979 and is seen outside The Lamb in the High Street during November 1992. By this time, the pair were regarded as dual-purpose vehicles although both had recovered seating. Ironically the pair remained united after disposal from Colchester, initially with Midland Fox and later Company Coaches of Pontefract, finally going for scrap when 22 years old.

GR Mills (3)

Inter-Town Service

Although CBT did not now operate on Sundays, special timetables were operated all day on Good Friday 17 April 1987. The following day saw the introduction of a new, somewhat controversial, Saturday only service between Colchester and Ipswich via Lawford and Brantham crossing the Orwell Bridge and along Nacton Road to the Tower Ramparts Bus Station. The service, numbered 25, ran every two hours and was to have been operated jointly with Ipswich Buses but this other local authority owned company withdrew following pressure from Eastern Counties. The latter operator then commenced a Colchester local service on Saturdays from 4 July 1987 between the Bus Station and St Michael's running just ahead of service 4A. CBT responded to this by adding additional journeys from 18 July 1987 to provide a ten-minute service to St Michael's. Initially passenger loadings on service 25 were reasonably good but suffered when Eastern Counties introduced a limited stop service between Colchester and Ipswich from 31 October 1987. Service 25 was withdrawn after operation on Saturday 19 December 1987 and Eastern Counties subsequently withdrew their competing services, thus ending a little local confrontation.

A further rural bus service, 77, was introduced on 7 May 1987 between Great Tey and Coggeshall on Thursdays. This was operated under contract to Essex County Council and replaced journeys previously operated by Hedingham Omnibuses, which in turn had gained the market day working with the acquisition of the C & R coach business at Little Tey.

Monday 22 June 1987 saw the introduction of new limited stop service X4 between Greenstead and the Town Centre operating non-stop between Greenstead roundabout and the top of East Hill. This service operated about hourly on Mondays to Fridays with four off-peak journeys projected beyond Greenstead via St Johns and Tyehurst to Highwoods (Tesco). The service was not a success and lasted until 31 December 1987.

Express Service Workings

Meanwhile two Leyland Tiger coaches (103 and 104) were acquired from West Riding and used on another experiment of providing services to destinations further afield. During the summer school holidays in 1987, express services to Great Yarmouth (on Tuesdays - X21), Brighton (Wednesdays - X23) and Southend (Thursdays - X22) were operated from 28 July to 3 September. No prior booking was necessary and the response was overwhelming, particularly to Great Yarmouth. The experiment was continued further for Christmas shoppers from 7 November with day trips to Norwich, Milton Keynes and Brent Cross, and a regular Wednesday service (X24) to Romford starting at Highwoods operated until 19 December 1987.

Back on Track

The Sunday depot closure was to be short lived. The company won a contract with British Rail - Network South East to provide rail replacement services on Sunday mornings and early afternoons between Colchester and Shenfield from 11 October 1987 to 15 May 1988 which required 18 buses. The service was extended on five Sundays in January and February to Clacton and Walton which required another eight buses with the extension running all day.

Further contracts followed as CBT gained a reputation for prompt turnouts at short notice at almost anytime of the day or night with buses sometimes reaching London Liverpool Street or Norwich at the other end of the line

Stormy Day

The now famous "near" hurricane of 16 October 1987 caused considerable disruption to bus services with CBT not venturing onto the streets until 10.00hrs and then there were a number of diversions for the rest of the day particularly for the Lexden Road routes due to fallen tree branches which littered the highway.

Odd Man In The Fleet

An unusual bus, for Colchester, was acquired on 18 December 1987 in the form of a standard Greater Manchester Leyland Atlantean with handsome Park Royal body to replace a Bristol RE (21) which had been written off after a serious accident. The Atlantean initially operated in Greater Manchester orange with the brown skirt painted crimson before being repainted into fleet colours.

Revisions introduced on 4 January 1988 included the withdrawal of limited stop service X4 but an increase in frequency of service 31 to half hourly on Mondays to Fridays although the section of route between Town Centre and General Hospital was withdrawn. Services 9/9A were revised at Lexden to run as a loop around Home Farm instead of terminating at Halstead Road Corner. The Saturday service to and from St Michael's (4A) was reduced to four buses per hour and the buses used to operate a half-hourly 2B via Tyehurst to Highwoods similar to Mondays to Fridays from 26 March 1988.

To add to the Sunday operations, the company then won a contract with Essex County Council to provide service 601 between Colchester and Saffron Walden from 27 March to 23 October 1988 as part of the Sunday Saver Network. The service ran every two hours via West Bergholt, Wormingford, Bures, Sudbury, Long Melford, Cavendish, Clare, Baythorne End, Haverhill, Castle Camps and Ashdon and required two vehicles, normally the Leyland Leopards 101/2

SECOND-HAND DOUBLE DECKERS
51: MVK538R

Seen entering St Botolphs Circus (via what later became a bus only lane) during November 1989. The fleetname below the waist was to allow a large clear area of panelling between the decks windows for advertising. The building to the right was the Colchester B.T. administration offices from May 1989 to February 1994.

THREE OF A KIND

51-3: MVK538/46/48R:

Three Leyland Atlanteans were acquired from Tyne & Wear in 1983; which introduced Alexander bodywork into the town fleet for the first time. New as H48/31D all three were converted to H48/34F in Newcastle prior to despatch to Colchester. The nearside staircase panel can be clearly seen in this line-up in Colchester bus station during December 1985.

ODD MAN

Leyland Atlantean/Park Royal. When CBT needed an instant replacement for a badly damaged Bristol RE, there was a prolific supply of ex Manchester buses rendered surplus by a huge number of operators competing in the city after de-regulation. 54: XJA517L was initially operated in Greater Manchester Transport as acquired orange and white with a crimson skirt as illustrated above leaving the bus station in January 1988 bound for Myland Hospital (built as an isolation ward, later eye special facility and finally demolished to make way for the Highwoods development.)

Right: Freshly repainted into CBT fleet livery 54 is seen posed up in the bus station during March 1988 for PSV Circle members. The parking charges then were £1 for '3 hours' or £5 for an 'all-day' stay. Inflation has increased somewhat since then.

GR Mills (4)

Excursions

A programme of day excursions was operated between 3 July and 18 September 1988 which included the express services to Great Yarmouth, Brighton and Southend but prior booking was required to prevent any embarassing overloads. Again success was recorded and the programme was extended until 17 December 1988.

Minibuses

After very careful consideration and deliberation the Board of Directors decided that the fleet should include a small number of mini - or midi - buses to develop new or enhance existing services and so an order was placed for five MCW Metroriders, four with 31 bus seats and one with 29 dual purpose seats. The vehicles should have been delivered for a service revision starting on 3 October 1988. In the event the new buses were late on delivery and MCW provided a number of demonstration vehicles and two Metroriders from Northumbria. The changes to bus services were again extensive. Service 2 was extended beyond Myland Hospital via Mill Road, Severalls Lane and Brinkley Lane to Highwoods to form a circular service. 2A was re-routed to run the whole length of Eastwood Drive in Highwoods. 3 was extended beyond Barnhall to Middlewick (Abbots Road) and returned via Old Heath Post Office as a new 3A through to Longridge Park thus increasing the frequency to every 30 minutes, the buses then continuing onto service 31 - the operation requiring four Metroriders. The Saturday timetable on service 4/4A reverted back to the original frequency before the hostilities with Eastern Counties. One journey per hour on service 5A was diverted away from Myland Hospital to run via Defoe Crescent and Nayland Road to Horkesley Heath (Malvern Way) and numbered 5B. At Stanway most service 5/5A/5B journeys were curtailed at Five Ways as services 9/9A were revised to run on beyond Home Farm via Lexden and then Beacon End (9) or New Farm Road and Five Ways (9A) to the Tollgate Shopping Centre.

Gain From Went's

Previously from 5 September 1988 the morning peak journey from Boxted commenced operation by CBT under contract to Essex County Council having been withdrawn commercially by Went's Coaches. This service was numbered 80. The Saturday service 76 to Rowhedge and Fingringhoe was also operated, but on a temporary basis, under contract to Essex County Council between 5 November and 31 December 1988.

Admin Moves Again

When the Company was formed in 1986 the Borough Council indicated its intention to redevelop the Osborne Street offices site. The proposed construction of a multi-storey car park meant CBT vacating the offices and premises at 26 St Botolph's Street, just across the road, were transferred to CBT and a suitable conversion took place. After much preparation the move was made over the weekend of 30 April - 1 May 1989.

Open - Topper 2

Meanwhile up at Magdalen Street work had been carried out to convert Leyland Atlantean 55 (JHK495N) to open top to replace 48 (YWC648F), which had been sold at the end of 1988, ready for the Circular Tour operation in the summer.

After a period of expansion of the bus services it became necessary to reduce costs which was reflected in the changes introduced on 5 June 1989. The ten minutes frequency on services 2/2A/2B was reduced to fifteen minutes with service 2B reduced to some Monday to Friday peak journeys. The timetable for midi-bus service 3/3A was reduced to hourly between North Station and Longridge Park as was service 31 between Longridge Park and town centre. Service 5A was extended beyond Myland Hospital to Highwoods but late evening buses were withdrawn. Service 9A was withdrawn from the General Hospital and instead terminated at Highwoods but re-routed via Tyehurst as partial replacement for service 2B. The Boxted journey on service 80 was incorporated into service 2. Service 5A was again changed from 20 November 1989 when it was re-routed via Severalls Park industrial estate on the way to and from Highwoods. Service 9A was re-routed along the whole length of Wheatfield Road at New Farm, Stanway from 4 December 1989.

The difficulties with the Travelcard scheme on journeys provided by the operators under contract to Essex County Council were resolved and Travelcards became valid on these journeys from 18 August 1989.

CBT Coachways Formed

A full excursions programme was operated throughout 1989 with considerable success and private hire revenue continued to increase. The Board of Directors thus considered the establishment of a separate coach unit and after much discussion CBT Coachways was launched on 7 February 1990. Two new Dennis Javelin coaches with Duple bodies were delivered in January and painted in a special livery of white and blue. The two Tiger coaches (103/4), a Metrorider (11) and an Olympian (46) were also repainted into Coachways livery. Two further new coaches - Volvo B10M with Hungarian built Ikarus bodies a rare purchase for a municipal operation - were delivered in October. As well as the then established excursions programme an extended tours programme was launched for the Autumn and a more extensive programme to venues in Europe introduced for 1991.

Went's Coaches deregistered the evening peak journey to Boxted and consequently a service 8 journey was extended beyond Severalls with effect from 2 January 1990, with financial support from Essex County Council. The journey was numbered 8B.

TWO COACHES FOUR LIVERIES
103: OHE274X

Top left: A pair of five year old Leyland Tigers with Duple Dominant IV bodies were acquired from West Riding in National Travel East bland white. Promptly repainted into cream and red as shown departing Colchester bus station in July 1987 on hire to Cedrics, Wivenhoe bound for a Genesis concert at Wembley.

Centre left: back in Colchester Borough Transport bus livery seen on arrival at Wembley Stadium in April 1997 with Bob Russell, then Colchester's future MP on a front passenger seat. The yellow diamond plaque in the front window is somewhat inappropriate as the coach party are about to watch Colchester United FC rather than attend a political rally!

Top right: Following on from the formation of CBT Coachways the pair were painted in an attractive white and blue livery with the bold gold CBT lettering. Seen in Witham on a Sunday in March 1990 working on rail replacement duties for British Rail Inter-City services.

Centre right: Freshly repainted into Arriva livery in February 2000 seen on Abbey Field, part of the town's extensive garrison prior to conveying military personnel to Salisbury Plain MoD area.

The initial coach fleet lined up at the Magdalen Street depot in September 1988.

Left to right: 104/3/1/2
The two Leyland Tigers with Duple Dominant IV coachwork blend in well with the two Leyland Leopards with Duple Dominant II bodies. Note: 103/4 have the Colchester Borough Transport lettering across the front panel, lost on first repaint, regained on second livery style (see photos above).

GR Mills (5)

New Ticket Issuing Style

The Almex ticket machines which had been introduced in 1971 were replaced by the latest electronic technology, Wayfarer Mark 3, from 15 October 1990. It has to be said it was not without its problems and although somewhat frustrating did cause s̶o̶m̶e̶ ̶ ̶ ̶ ̶ ̶sement when one day some machines issued extra long tickets! The Board threatened to remo̶ ̶ ̶ ̶ ̶ ̶ ̶ ̶ ̶ ̶ially it settled down after much work by technicians.

...passengers travelling by bus resulted in another revision to services from 28 October ... the new link road between Mill Road and Highwoods, subsequently named Brinkley ...ced to hourly throughout and extended beyond Middlewick to Old Heath (Cheveling ...esley Heath were re-routed to Highwoods as 5A and replaced by a diversion of ...eralls to Horkesley Heath (as 8A). At Stanway most service 5A buses were again ...gate as services 9/9A on the Home Farm - Tollgate section were withdrawn. The ...ge Park was withdrawn and replaced by a diversion of service 9A from Harwich ...red 39 and linked to service 3. A further attempt to deploy the midibuses for the ...ntroduction of service 21 between Tollgate, New Farm, Prettygate, Drury Road and ...tes on Monday, Tuesday, Wednesday and Friday mornings for shoppers. As part ...ourneys were altered to operate under contract to Essex County Council, and the ...en Tollgate and town centre.

...al of 60 vehicles in 1988 and stood at 58 in 1991. The conditions at the garage ... formation land to the east of No 2 garage had been acquired which enabled a ...way through from No 2 garage and a separate exit on to Magdalen Street. More ...n Street to the west of No 1 garage were demolished and the workshop behind ...king space, mainly for the coaches.

...een well received by passengers or staff and had encountered engineering ...ose of them to Strathclyde Buses in February 1991. In their place came two ...r units which were delivered on Friday 8 February, a day on which no CBT ... The new buses entered service the following week in white livery pending ...e materialised as Colchester Mortgage Centre and Foulkes Electrical. Two ...ed.

...riday in previous years was not operated in 1991, it falling to Essex County ...bles. This arrangement continued in subsequent years.

...gradually developing a computer scheduling programme tailored to CBT's ...luable for the many service revisions as well as the rail replacement

...o sets of service revisions took effect in 1991. Service 74A to Wivenhoe was withdrawn after operation on 8 June following introduction of an increased service operated by Eastern National. However CBT provided the third bus on services 6/6A to Old Heath and Rowhedge from 10 June and Eastern National withdrew their bus on this route two weeks later. Now that was a coincidence!

Other changes from 10 June 1991 involved timetable alterations in the peak periods in an endeavour to overcome the increasing traffic congestion problems. Service 21 was re-routed via Home Farm, the timetable having been previously revised to operate hourly on Monday to Friday mornings from 7 January.

The second changes to timetable and routes took place on 2 September 1991. Service 3 was withdrawn apart from some peak period journeys for commuters between Longridge Park - North Station - Town Centre. Service 39 was also withdrawn and in replacement some peak journeys on a new service 1B between Longridge Park and Town Centre via Harwich Road were introduced together with a new hourly service 3A between Greenstead Roundabout and Town Centre via Longridge Park, Harwich Road, Cowdray Avenue and North Station. Barnhall and Middlewick were served by diverting part of service 6A to and from Old Heath, these journeys being numbered 6B. Service 9 was reduced to a handful of peak journeys and service 9A was revised to run hourly between Highwoods and Home Farm and then on to Tollgate via Dugard Avenue and New Farm to replace service 21 which was withdrawn.

From the same date a Day Rover Ticket for £2 was introduced as part of a general fares revision and was valid on CBT buses in an area corresponding with the inner area of the Colchester Travelcard.

Service 5A was re-routed in the Severalls Park Industrial Estate via The Crescent from 20 January 1992 and the Saturday service between the Town Centre and Highwoods was reinstated but ran via Brinkley Grove Road on this day. From the same date most service 8 buses were re-routed to Horkesley Heath as 8A to provide a half-hourly frequency.

COLCHESTER BOROUGH TRANSPORT

SATURDAY LINK COLCHESTER – IPSWICH

A new Service 25 on SATURDAYS will link COLCHESTER (Bus Station) and IPSWICH (Tower Ramparts Bus Station) running via Parsons Heath, Ardleigh, Lawford, Cattawade, Brantham, Tattingstone, Orwell Bridge, Ipswich Airport and Nacton Road, about every 2 hours.
Single, Day Return and Family Fares will be available.

FOR FULL DETAILS SEE LEAFLET OBTAINABLE FROM OSBORNE STREET ENQUIRY OFFICE, TOWN HALL AND TOURIST INFORMATION OFFICE IN COLCHESTER, AND IPSWICH BUS ENQUIRY OFFICE AND TOURIST INFORMATION OFFICE IN IPSWICH.

Take the Scenic Bus Route between Colchester and Ipswich

Starting Saturday 18 April 1987

COLCHESTER BOROUGH TRANSPORT LIMITED
Osborne Street
Colchester CO2 7DP

THREE DEPARTURES PER DAY

COLCHESTER BOROUGH TRANSPORT LIMITED

Take a trip on the

GUIDED SIGHTSEEING TOUR OF COLCHESTER BY BUS

(usually an open top double decker)

28 June to 4 September 1993
Mondays to Saturdays
(Except Bank Holidays)
at 11.30 a.m., 2.00 and 3.30 p.m.

CASTLE PARK (Main Gate by War Memorial)

**No prior booking needed
Just come along and pay on the bus
Tour lasts about 75 minutes**

FARES
Adults   £3.00
OAPS   £1.50
Children £1.50

Top left: 11: F111NPU the only one of the five Metroriders delivered with dual purpose type seating. Delivered in standard livery 11 was only 17 months old when repainted into CBT Coachways white and blue. Seen outside the Town Hall in High Street on the first outing after the colour change in April 1990.

Top right: 46: F246MTW one of the third pair of Leyland Olympians fitted with high speed back axles delivered to Colchester, both new with dual purpose seating, ideally suited for coach work. Freshly repainted into CBT Coachways livery as shown in April 1990 crossing Headgate Corner bound for Stanway on normal bus duties.

CBT*Coachways*

February 1990 to November 1993

107: H107JAR A very unusual purchase for a municipal operator was an all foreign built product. The Volvo B10M chassis was less startling than the Hungarian body built by Ikarus in Budapest. The mainly steel body was so heavy that day trips to France for duty-free goods was not practical. Seen on the A12 at Marks Tey on a Titan Tours working in November 1990.

Bottom left: 105: G105AVX Marked a return to Dennis chassis after 60 years, with a pair of Javelins with Duple 320 coachwork. Seen leaving Colchester's North Station during February 1990 on rail replacement work; within 4 years the pair left the town's fleet indefinitely.

Bottom right: J109WVW a stock Leyland Tiger/Plaxton Paramount was the last new coach ever supplied to the borough. Seen when brand new at Friday Woods in September 1991 the smart vehicle was only operated for 2 years before moving on to the London Borough of Havering at Hornchurch.   GR Mills (5)

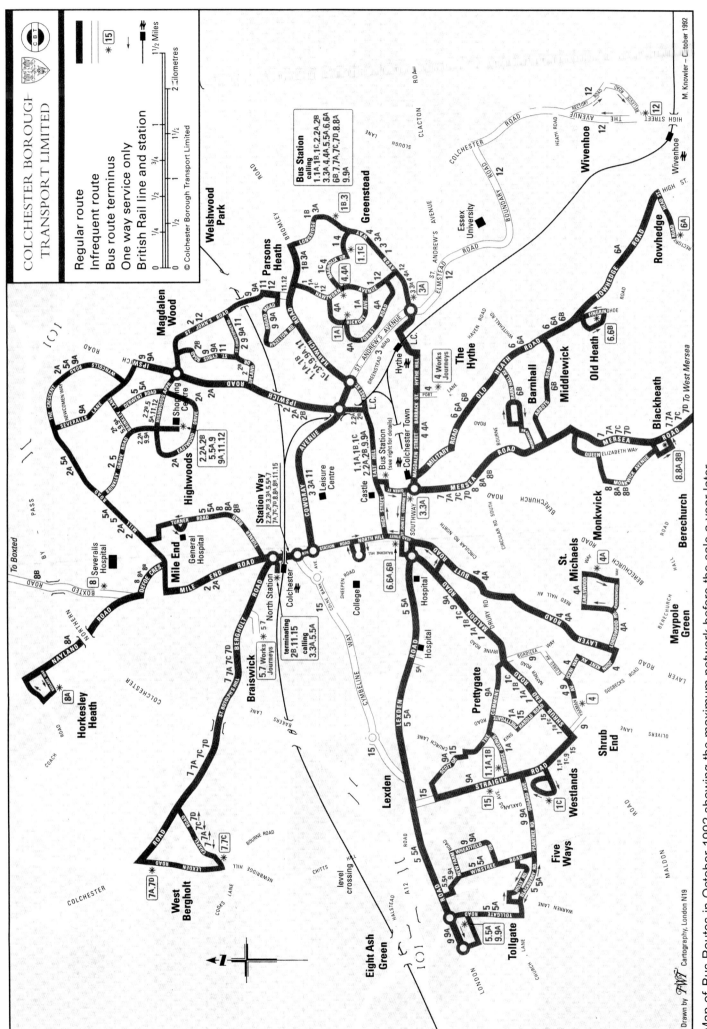

Map of Bus Routes in October 1992 showing the maximum network before the sale a year later

Supermarket Runs End

There was some disappointment when Tesco announced that they would be terminating the contract for the provision of the free bus services to and from the Highwoods store as part of their general policy to withdraw such services - the services ceased on 3 April 1992. As part replacement a new service 12 from Wivenhoe to Highwoods via Greenstead was introduced on 8 April. It ran Wednesday and Friday mornings and was free for the first two weeks pending registration becoming effective.

Tendered Services Lost

Most of the local bus services provided under contract to Essex County Council were due for retendering in 1992 and in anticipation that there would be some strong competition a decision was made to register the commuter services 11 and 15 to and from North Station as a commercial operation - neither service actually requiring peak vehicles (because operation was before 0800hrs and after 1800hrs). As expected services 10, 13, 14, 16, 75, 82A and 83 were lost to other operators.

Westlands Served - Amid Objections

The resulting major service revision started on 7 September 1992 but the opportunity was taken to introduce some improvements and new facilities. Requests had been received from some residents for a bus service to Westlands estate off Straight Road in Shrub End and when it was discovered that CBT would be introducing a new service a majority of residents on the estate formed a residents association to protest in the strongest terms. Nevertheless, the new service 1C was introduced, which, with a revised 1/1A timetable, increased the frequency along Shrub End Road and Harwich Road to every 10 minutes. Amongst other changes the remaining service 5 journeys via Dugard Avenue were re-routed as 5A via Beacon End and the number 5 was used to denote journeys running via Brinkley Grove Road to and from Highwoods (5A journeys ran via Severalls Park). Services 9/9A were altered again with an improved service between the Town Centre and Tollgate. The Wednesday operation on service 12 (Wivenhoe - Highwoods) was withdrawn so it ran on Fridays only.

Gloomy Clouds Gather

The Board of Directors was concerned at the worsening financial situation of the company. The continuing economic recession had badly affected the company and at the end of the 1992 financial year a deficit of £386,223 had accumulated. It was therefore necessary to make further adjustments to services in 1993. The first revision took place on 8 March when services 1/1A/1B/1C were rescheduled, maintaining the 10 minute frequency but providing one bus per hour via Longridge on Service 1B, service 1C via Westlands was withdrawn. Service 3A was also withdrawn. Services 5/5A were curtailed at Five Ways instead of continuing to Tollgate at Stanway. All the service 8A journeys were numbered 8. Service 9 was revised to provide an hourly service between the Town Centre and Tollgate via Shrub End and the Westlands loop whilst service 9A ran hourly between Highwoods and Tollgate. Evening services were again revised by arrangement with Essex County Council. The Friday only service 12 was withdrawn after operation on 7 April 1993.

Mass Rail Workings

Meanwhile preparations were being made for a major rail replacement service at Shenfield during the Easter weekend in 1993. However the work was postponed until August but CBT was contracted by Capital Citybus to provide four buses on a replacement service for the London Docklands Light Railway between Stratford and Canary Wharf on 13 and 14 April. The resignalling work at Shenfield was carried out over the late summer Bank Holiday weekend 26-31 August. The bus requirement reached a peak of 55 vehicles on the Monday of which CBT provided 27, others coming from Capital Citybus, Southend Transport and Stephensons of Rochford. In addition a coach service was operated between Witham and London - this was sub-contracted to Eastern National who enlisted the services of 16 other operators.

Eastern National Attack

During the summer of 1993 the Company produced a recovery plan which was audited independently by accountants appointed by the Company's Bankers. The plan was approved and envisaged a further revision of services in November which would see the peak vehicle requirement reduced from 40 to 34. It emerged, however, in late August that Eastern National (then owned by the Badgerline Group) had registered three high-frequency minibus routes in direct competition with CBT from 4 October and a further three routes with conventional buses from 17 October. CBT's proposals for 1 November were hastily changed and three new services were registered in token retaliation: Colchester - Braintree (70), Colchester - Weeley - Clacton (109) and Colchester - St Osyth - Clacton (174). Each was to operate hourly but in the event the Traffic Commissioners later accepted cancellation of these registrations and the services were never operated.

LAST ORDERS

Top: 41: C41HHJ

The first of nine Leyland Olympians supplied to CBT these ousted the remaining PDR1/1's and the oldest AN68's. The new breed proved to be excellent vehicles ideally suited to the longer stage routes and private hire. The air suspension and high speed back axles were used to full advantage particularly on rail replacement duties. Seen crossing the Stroud causeway which regularly floods, with Bob Franklin at the wheel en route from Mersea Island back to town during December 1992; The service was withdrawn in November 1993.

Centre left: 11: F111NPU numerically the first of 5 Metroriders new in 1988 to ward off any competition from the numerous operators serving the town. Seen in Military Road (back of depot) during December 1988 (Gunsmiths in background later became a fish and chip shop!). In original livery, repainted into CBT Coachways in April 1990 but sold to Strathclyde ten months later together with rest of batch.

Centre right: 48: H48MJN one of final trio of new Olympians supplied in 1991; was repainted blue and yellow, despatched to Southend in December 1993 for use on the London service. Returned to Colchester in February 1994 as the bus seats were unsuitable on coach workings. Seen in Tufnell Way on a lunchtime service from Woods (fan manufacturers) factory still in full Southend Transport livery and fleet number 448 on waist. See front cover for photo of twin bus 49 in Arriva livery.

FINAL NEW BUS

27: K27EWC

The last of 14 Leyland Lynx supplied new to CBT. Thus together with the 9 Olympians; 5 Metroriders and 5 coaches CBT entered the nineties with a *very* modern fleet. The smart Lynx II is seen in Newcastle Avenue, Westlands in May 1993 advertising CBT Coachways on the roofcants. After the CBT take-over by British Bus all 14 of the Lynx went to Crosville Wales in 1994.

GR Mills (4)

West Mersea Abandoned

A service revision was implemented on 1 November which saw services 7/7A withdrawn between Blackheath and West Mersea. The revised service operated half-hourly between West Bergholt and Blackheath being interworked with service 8 which was extended beyond Monkwick to Blackheath. Service 9 was completely withdrawn leaving an hourly service 9A between Highwoods and Tollgate, with an extension on Mondays to Fridays to start at Severalls Park. Timetable revisions were made to other services but basic frequencies were retained.

It should also be recorded that the school service 16 between Old Heath and St Helena School, which had been lost to Hedingham Omnibuses in September 1992, was transferred back to CBT from 7 September 1993 at Hedingham's request, following County Council approval. Consequently two Hedingham double-deckers, former Blackpool Atlanteans previously with Norfolks of Nayland, were on hire until 17 November.

Entire Operation Sold

With intense competition and a worsening financial situation, the Borough Council was forced to consider the future of its Bus Company and appointed Price Waterhouse to investigate and submit an urgent report. The recommendation was to sell to the private sector and a number of potential purchasers were approached. The British Bus group emerged as the preferred bidder early in November (they had already purchased Southend Transport earlier in the year). British Bus made it clear that the take over would involve a number of conditions being met which would affect the staff. Discussions with Trade Union representatives took place but the terms were initially rejected. The Borough Council confirmed that if agreement on conditions could not be met then receivers would have to be appointed. Further meetings took place and finally on 11 November the staff reluctantly accepted. The Borough Council finalised the sale to British Bus on 22 November 1993 for the sum of £1 but the new owners took on the considerable outstanding debts.

CBT Coachways Ceased

By then Eastern National had registered the remaining routes so that in January 1994 wherever a CBT bus would run, an Eastern National one preceded it. However British Bus did not react to this and concentrated on getting CBT back on its feet. A new Manager was appointed but overall control passed to London & Country at Reigate. The first event was the closure of CBT Coachways and the removal of five coaches in the first week of new ownership. The new pay and conditions agreement was implemented and a number of administration staff were made redundant.

Whilst this upheaval was going on, CBT managed to supply three buses to operate between Debden and Chingford on 25-29 November following a major breakdown on the London Underground as well as weekend rail replacement services.

Newest Saloons Depart

In January 1994, what became an ongoing reshuffle of vehicles commenced. Two Leyland Olympians were transferred to Midland Fox in exchange for Leyland National 2s. Several more of these were to come to Colchester during the year as all the Leyland Lynxes were gradually transferred to Crosville Wales. Perhaps more significant was the fact that this marked a turning point - no more new buses were to be delivered to Magdalen Street.

Admin Back to Base

February saw the closure of the St Botolph's Street offices and the transfer of functions back to Magdalen Street. However Travelcard sales and bus enquiries were dealt with at A & O Travel which had opened at 32 St Botolph's Street owned by the former manager of CBT Coachways. This business was later acquired by TravelStyle of Chesterfield in December 1994.

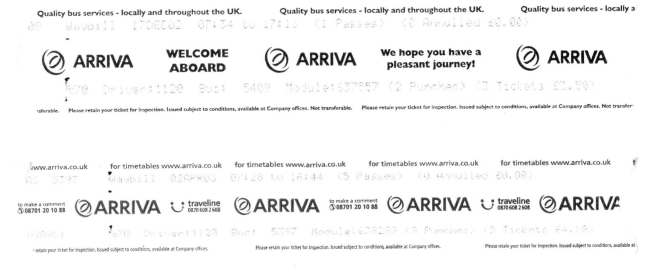

Wayfarer tickets issued as driver's waybills

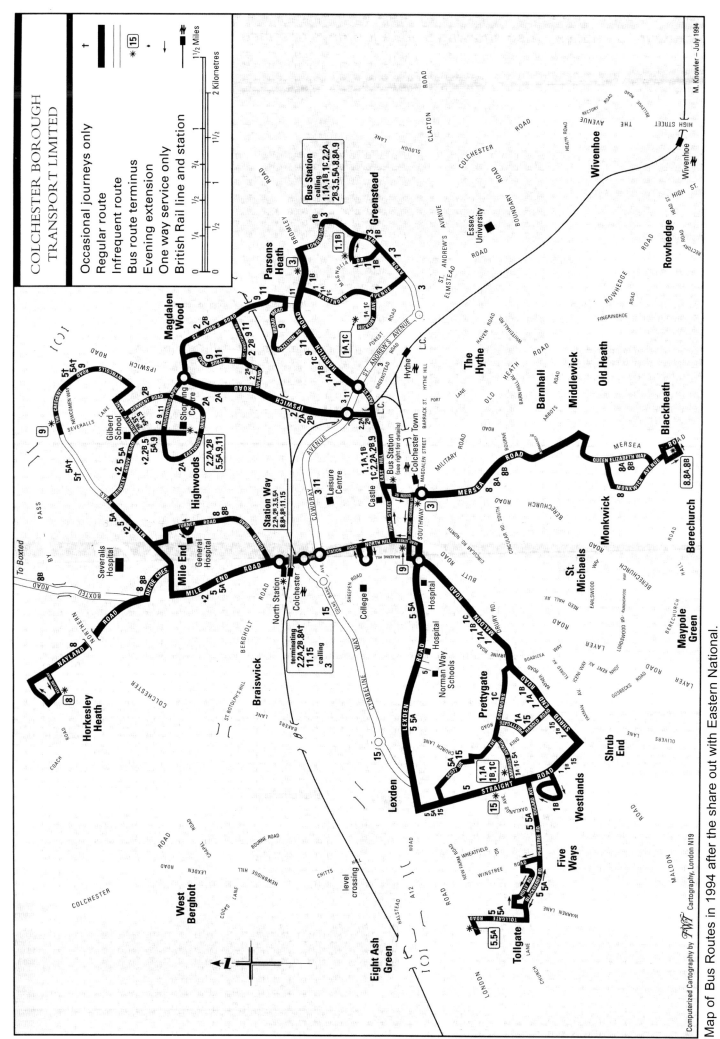

Map of Bus Routes in 1994 after the share out with Eastern National.

Computerized Cartography by TWT Cartography, London N19

62

Peace Declared

In March it emerged that discussions had been held with Eastern National to end the head-to-head conflict and arrangements made to share out the Colchester area routes. The revised services were introduced on 25 April 1994. CBT required 29 buses at peak periods and 24 during the off-peak, this gave a fleet requirement of 35 buses, 2 coaches and one open-top bus (total 38). The new commercial network was as follows:

Service	Route	Basic weekday frequency
1/1A/1B/1C	Greenstead - Longridge Park (1B) - Harwich Road - Town Centre - Maldon Road - The Commons (1C) or Leather Bottle (1/1B) or Prettygate (1A/1C) - Westlands (1B) - Ambrose Avenue	every 7/8 minutes
2/2A/2B	Highwoods - Derwent Road (2B) or Eastwood (2A) - St Johns (2/2B) - Ipswich Road - Town Centre - North Station	every 10 minutes
3	Longridge Park - Town Centre - North Station	Monday to Friday peak journeys
5/5A	Highwoods - Mile End - North Station - Town Centre – Lexden - Straight Road (5) or Home Farm and Ambrose Avenue (5A) - Dugard Avenue - Five Ways – Tollgate	every 30 minutes - see also 65/65A
8/8A/8B	Monkwick - Silver Oyster (8A) - Mersea Road - Town Centre - North Station - General Hospital - Horkesley Heath (8) two peak hour journeys to/from Boxted (8B)	every 15/30 minutes
9	Town Centre - Harwich Road - Bridgebrook - St Johns – Tyehurst - Highwoods, extended hourly to Severalls Park (Monday to Friday)	every 30 minutes
11	Highwoods - St Johns - North Station	peak journeys
15	Lexden - Prettygate - North Station	peak journeys

The former CBT routes operated by Eastern National were as follows:

64/64A (ex 4/4A)	Greenstead - Hythe - Town Centre - Layer Road - Shrub End or St Michaels	every 7/8 minutes
65/65A (ex 5/5A)	Highwoods - General Hospital - North Station - Town Centre - Lexden - Beacon End - Five Ways - Tollgate (coordinated with 5/5A)	every 30 minutes
66/66A/66A (ex 6/6A/6B)	Town Centre - Old Heath – Rowhedge	every 7/8 minutes
67/67A (ex 7/7A)	West Bergholt - North Station - Town Centre - Blackheath -- West Mersea	every 30 minutes

It should be noted that in most cases there were more buses on each route than prior to the competition but less than the combined figure operated by both companies during the "bus war".

The 90th Anniversary was recorded in July 1984 by painting Leyland Atlantean no 84, rather than the more obvious bus 90, into a livery similar to that applied to the buses in the 1930s. 84 was used because it was receiving attention in the paintshop at the time.

Brightlingsea School

A contract to convey a large number of school children from Wivenhoe to Brightlingsea (Colne High School) resulted in a new group of services (numbered 31) being registered from 6 September 1994. As a result, six Atlanteans were transferred from London & Country, for a time these operated in the distinctive green livery before being repainted. These services operated for four years when the contract was lost to Cedrics of Wivenhoe, the principal long term contractor.

Peak hour service 3 was withdrawn after operation on 1 September 1995. Commuter services 11 and 15 were also deregistered but these were regained on contract to the County Council from 4 September together with the West Bergholt to Stanway school service 17, previously operated by Hedingham Omnibuses.

Midicoach Reintroduced

An unusual vehicle was transferred to Magdalen Street in April 1996 in the form of a Mercedes-Benz midi-coach, its prime purpose being to operate tours of Constable Country which started in London.

Alterations to services introduced on 29 July 1996 saw service 1B diverted via Bridgebrook and service 2B diverted via Tyehurst (again) as part replacement of the half hourly service 9 which was revised to run as a circular service on Mondays to Fridays with two/three journeys each way from the Town Centre via Bridgebrook, Tyehurst, Eastwood, Highwoods, Severalls Park, General Hospital, North Station to town centre. Services 5 and 5A were simplified to run half-hourly as service 5 via Home Farm, Heath Road and Straight Road at Lexden.

25: EON825V

The initial replacement for the CBT Lynx seconded to North Wales were seven Leyland National 2 models transferred from Midland Fox. Arriving in the town in red and yellow the batch were all repainted in the CBT paintshop. Looking well for a 15 year old bus 25 is seen passing the Prettygate shops during July 1995. All but one passed to Supreme Coaches of Hadleigh, Essex, with a depot on Whitehall Industrial Estate, in Colchester some worked in the town again albeit in a new livery.

LNC463: NWO463R

Leyland National Urban bus new to National Welsh, Cardiff in 1977 as a standard bus, upgraded in 1992 for Guildford & West Surrey Buses before transfer to Colchester in 1996. From 23 July 1997 to 3 September 1997 worked a special Fun Bus Service from town to Greenstead, St Johns, Highwoods and Turner Road to Leisureworld as seen in the bus station in the first week of operation; about to perform another journey. Sponsored by Colchester Borough Council, SGR Radio and MacDonalds.

NATIONAL GAIN MONOPOLY WITH SALOONS

351: NIW6511 (ex LPR938P)

One of a second wave of Leyland Nationals, were 8 drafted in from London & Country in 1996 rendered surplus by Addlestone (WY) garage following the loss of tendered services 116/7 Brentford to Staines which passed to London United & Armchair respectively. The 1967 vehicle had been extensively upgraded to Greenway specification in 1993 by East Lancashire, i.e. new front, new panelling, new seating and a new Gardner power unit. Seen in Osborne Street, crew change stop, outside Gala Bingo hall, freshly repainted into CBT livery during September 1996.

GR Mills (3)

Top left: 64: PUF131M a 1974 Leyland Atlantean/Park Royal originally 1 of a batch of 14 new to Southdown MS which later passed to Ribble. The 20 year old looks well although accident damage to the front upper deck whilst with one of the previous operators has created a very non standard rebuild in this September 1994 view in Hickory Avenue, Greenstead.

Top right: 65: MUA865P a 1976 Leyland Atlantean new to Yorkshire Woollen with a Park Royal body destroyed by fire in 1979. Rebodied by Roe in 1981; later worked for BTS, Borehamwood, and London Pride. The much travelled bus is seen departing Ambrose Avenue in October 1994. Sold for preservation when 21 years old.

Centre left: 66: RFR416P one of four Leyland Atlantean/ECW new to Ribble fitted into the fleet well as the same vintage as 61-66 disposed of in1991/2. They varied in having a higher driving position.

LONDON & COUNTRY 'DECKER VARIETY

Centre right: 70: RFR421P all 4 of the 'Ribble' AN68's entered service in Colchester in London & Country duo-green as portrayed in this action shot on Maldon Road roundabout on Southway in September 1994.

Bottom left: 62: RCN96N one of a pair of 1974 Leyland Atlantean/Park Royal new to the NGT group in yellow livery as H45/28D rebuilt to single door in 1981. The twin PCN892M barely survived for 3 months whereas 62 was repainted and operated in town for a year as shown in Osborne Street, in March 1996.

Bottom right: 185: XPG185T the newest of the nine ex London & County Atlanteans drafted into CBT for operational use, had started life with LCBS. Seen at Magdalen Street depot in April 1996 freshly repainted. 78 and 86 can be seen at rest in the background.

GR Mills (6)

STORY OF BUS 60

Above: In Eurolines contract livery seen at Great Yarmouth, Beach Coach Station (ex M & GN railway terminus) during September 1986 working GreyGreen X35 from North London.

Top right: After the Cowie Group acquired County Bus, Harlow in February 1996; the batch all migrated into Essex by April 1997. Only 6 months later 60 was in Colchester still in Town Link hue as this October 1997 view passing St Botolphs Station shows.

60: B860XYR
Originally one of batch of seventeen Volvo B10M-61 (A855/6 UYM, B857-61 XYR) delivered to GreyGreen in 1984/5 with Plaxton Paramount 3500 C49FT bodywork. In 1992 most of the coach bodies were removed and re-bodied by East Lancs as d.d's; but seven received East Lancs B49F i.e. AB55/6 UYM and B857-61 XYR which were put to work on London Transport service 20 Walthamstow to Debden Station. After service in Colchester, 57-60 were sold to the Rapson Group to work in North Scotland in attractive Highland livery of two-tone blue.

Centre left: 60 representing the last batch of buses to be painted in CBT livery. Seen at work in The Commons passing Prettygate Shops on service 1C during March 1998.
Centre right: 60 as 3320 in Arriva livery approaching Fordham Memorial/Village Hall, during July 1999 in the final month of Arriva operation on service 82, an Essex CC tendered working from November 1997.

Right: 55: A855UYM The first CBT 55 not a unique bus. Unfortunately 58 was chosen to be route branded for service 3. Seen on rail replacement working twixt Marks Tey and Sudbury via Bures a regular commitment in November 1997.

GR Mills (5)

RE-BODIED COACHES

Control Changes

The Cowie Group purchased British Bus plc in August 1996 and in the following June, control of CBT passed to County Bus & Coach Co Ltd at Harlow. This resulted in former Grey-Green rebodied Volvo single-deckers, and later ex-London Metrobuses being transferred to Magdalen Street. In October 1997, the Cowie Group was renamed Arriva and in December, the first of the acquired Metrobuses appeared in the new Arriva livery. On 2 April 1998, Colchester Borough Transport Ltd was renamed Arriva Colchester Ltd. In a further reorganisation of the group, control passed to Arriva The Shires at Luton on 1 August 1998. The fleet was renumbered in January 1999 into a common series with Arriva Southend, Arriva The Shires and Arriva East Herts & Essex.

Further revisions to the services were made on 20 April 1998. These included the diversion of 1C via Bridgebrook instead of 1B, and the extension beyond North Station of one journey per hour on service 2 to Highwoods via the General Hospital and on service 2A to General Hospital. A new service 3 was introduced between Home Farm and General Hospital via Prettygate, Ambrose Avenue, Shrub End, Maldon Road and Town Centre running every seventy-five minutes. The circular journeys on service 9 were withdrawn thus reducing it to one journey each way between Town Centre and Highwoods at school times.

Essex County Council local bus service contracts gained in 1997 included the Sunday evening service on 78 between Colchester (General Hospital) and Brightlingsea which started on 30 March (this ran until 1 April 2002), the Monday to Saturday 66C circular from Colchester to Fingringhoe from 3 November (also until 1 April 2002); and some journeys on 82 between Colchester and Fordham which operated from 3 November 1997 until 2 August 1999.

Competition Intensified

Meanwhile on 29 June 1998, Eastern National, by then part of First Group, broke away from the joint timetable on services 5/65/65A by increasing the frequency of their 65/65A to every 20 minutes and introduced five low-floor Darts in First corporate livery. Arriva's response was to transfer four low-floor Darts, new in 1996, from Grays to Colchester for operation on service 5. First went on to improve their service even further by increasing the frequency to every 15 minutes from 2 April 2002 and again to every 12 minutes from 14 July 2003. Curiously Arriva's response to the latter increase was to transfer the only low-floor Darts, which normally ran on service 5, to Gillingham in Kent for a Park & Ride contract.

North Hill Bus Lane

Bus priority measures were introduced at Middleborough in March 1999 together with a southbound bus lane up North Hill. This of course (see the reference in 1977) caused much controversy and was removed in October 2003.

Some changes to services started on 22 March 1999 with service 3 revised to run hourly but between the Town Centre and Home Farm with a diversion via Westlands. Most service 8A buses were extended beyond the Town Centre via North Station to the General Hospital.

Demise of Standard 'Deckers

By October 1999 only three of the standard Leyland Atlantean/ECW buses, which had served Colchester so well, remained in the fleet. Their demise was mourned by forty-two local enthusiasts who took part in a "Farewell to the Atlanteans Tour" of Colchester routes on 5 December using bus 90 (then numbered 5320). All three Atlanteans were withdrawn in that month, 85 (5315), being the last to operate on 13 December 1999.

Further Essex County Council contract services started on 31 July 2000 including service 83 between Chappel and Colchester on Mondays to Fridays with one journey starting at Colne Engaine on Mondays and Mount Bures on Tuesdays (a Saturday service was added from 28 October 2002); a Saturday service on route 87 Dedham – Colchester; and a schooldays service 247 from Langham to Colchester with the return journey operating through to East Bergholt. A Monday to Friday peak service was added to the 87 from 8 January 2001 and service 247 was enhanced to Monday to Saturday operation from 9 December 2002.

Stansted Served

Another new Essex County Council contracted service, 133, commenced on 28 May 2000, running between Braintree and Stansted Airport every two hours on Sundays and Public Holidays. When Eastern National withdrew their Monday to Saturday service, Arriva introduced a two-hourly commercial service as replacement from 21 August with some journeys supported by Essex County Council and the British Airports Authority. Even though the route was remote from Magdalen Street, it appeared to work well and the frequency was increased to hourly from 8 January 2001. Some positioning journeys were registered between Colchester and Braintree (as service 70). Some early morning journeys on service 59 between Chelmsford and Harlow were also operated under contract to the County Council from Magdalen Street. Eastern National, who by then had replaced Eastern Counties on the Colchester - Ipswich service, withdrew this operation from 8 January 2001 and Arriva stepped in with a partial replacement between Colchester and East Bergholt. This service, numbered 194, ran generally every hour during Monday to Saturday daytime.

TIGERS BACK IN TOWN

Top left: 100: A250 SVW 1985 Leyland Tiger/Duple Caribbean was on loan to Colchester for numerous previous periods throughout the summer of 1994 in Southend Transport London Coachlink livery of blue and yellow as shown at the Leisure Centre, in Cowdray Avenue during November 1994. Top right: 100 was eventually officially transferred to Colchester in 1995 and repainted into CBT livery as seen at Parkeston Quay, Harwich working ship's crew transfers during August 1996. Centre left: 100 now Arriva 4310 sports a third livery whilst based in Colchester. The coach is seen waiting in Stanwell Street, official tour and excursion pick-up point in January 1999. Centre right: 4312 joined 4310 in late 1999 providing a pair of very unusual 57 seaters for school contract duties. Seen together in Mill Road on a private hire for Colchester Rugby Club to Bromley, Kent in October 2000.

PIONEER MIDI-BUS

123: H123WFM the first of some 20 Mercedes Benz which were to follow over the next six years; the only one not fitted with a destination display. Bottom left: On hire to Great Eastern Railway linking Manningtree with Ipswich involving passing under a very low bridge (only 10ft clearance) as shown in December 1996 driven by Dave King. Bottom right: Freshly repainted into Arriva livery seen in the Stanwell Street coach pick-up point before working a private hire in January 1998 again driven by Dave King!   GR Mills (6)

ARRIVA ARRIVES

Top left: 5366: EYE336V the first Metrobus, with claims in the local press that 20 more were to follow, but only 7 plus one for spares ever arrived! The bus was also the first in Arriva livery to operate in Colchester. Seen at Stanway, Tollgate outside Sainsburys bound for Asda Superstore in February 1998.

Top right: 5383: TPD123X the third of 3 Leyland Olympian/Roe drafted into Colchester when controlled by The Shires, Luton. Seen freshly repainted at work on service 3, normally provided by a midibus, in Newcastle Avenue, Westlands during May 2000.

Centre left: 5388: B189BLG a Leyland Olympian/lowheight ECW originally new to Crosville in 1985, but transferred from Southend. Unfortunately due to a premature engine failure the bus was withdrawn after only 3 months and hence never lost 'Serving Southend' fleetnames, as shown in May 2002 on layover.

Centre right: 5030: CBD904T the only Bristol VRT ever based in Magdalen Street, had an even shorter stay, only one month, the bus performed only one contract i.e. en route into Stanway School still shown on the destination blind in this No. 2 garage shot in February 2000.

THREE BIG UNS

Left: 613/617/614 G613/7/4 BPH 1989 Volvo Citybus/ East Lancs 88 seaters ideal for school contracts i.e. Thomas Lord Audley on the Monkwick Estate, to Mersea Island. Regular performers on service 8, normally always a double-decker allocation. The trio are seen at rest on a Saturday in March 2003 in the yard outside No. 2 garage.

GR Mills (5)

69

Top left: 3079: F151KGS One of two pairs of Volvo B10M with Plaxton Derwent II B54F. Two were new to Sampson Cheshunt whilst the second pair (as above) were new to Buffalo, Flitwick. 3079 is seen in High Street, (the colonnades of the Fire Office visible in the background) about to work the first journey in Colchester service in August 2000.

Top right: 3430: P430HVX the first of four Dennis Dart super low floor, drafted in to work service 5 as shown at the Tollgate terminus in June 1998. Five years later all 4 were despatched to Gillingham to work a Park & Ride service; thus eliminating low floor from the fleet!

Centre left: 2319: L613LVX one of a pair of Mercedes Benz with rare Dormobile of Folkestone B31F body which had a short stay in the town. Neil Crowther sets off from No. 1 garage for Dedham in June 2001.

Centre Right: One of a trio of Volvo B6/Alexander Dash B40F new to Clydeside Buses in 1994. Seen leaving Highwoods terminus in September 2001. Ironically the very location where an engine fire in the vehicle lead to a premature withdrawal from the fleet in June 2003.

Bottom left: 3335: H350PNO new to Wests of Woodford Green as H550AMT, later re-registered A19BUS and H20 BUS a 1991 Leyland Swift/Wadham Stringer Vanguard which spent most days at work on service 3 as seen in High Street, outside the Co-op Bank former Albert Hall (ex Repertory Theatre/Art Gallery) during March 2000.

Bottom right: H350PNO returns to town, briefly as a training bus, repainted white and grey, but retaining fleet no. 3335 in the bus station in August 2001. GR Mills (6)

ARRIVA SALOON SELECTION

Top left: 4339: K124TCP one of 4 Dutch built DAF SB 220 the first such for Colchester, but the Hungarian produced Ikarus bodies re-introduced the manufacturer to the town 7½ years after 107/8 coaches left. Seen passing Greyfriars (former County High School for Girls) at the top of East Hill during March 2001.

Top right: 3092: H923LOX a solitary Dennis Dart with rare Carlyle body spent a few months in Colchester in the winter of 2001/2. Seen in Queen Street departing the bus station during January 2002. Centre left: DS4: L506CPJ one of 8 Dennis Dart/East Lancs new to London & County 1994-6. Seen August 2003 passing Colchester Zoo at Stanway working service 92 from Tollesbury via Birch into Colchester.

Centre right: 201: L201YCU a solitary Volvo B6 with a Northern Counties Paladin B39F body originally one of 12 supplied to Kentish Bus in 1994. Transferred to Colchester as a low floor Dart replacement, seen at No. 2 depot yard prepared to work service 83 to Wakes Colne during July 2003. 3406: P326HVX rests in background.

Bottom left: 3342: H252GEV the return of the Lynx to Colchester after six years absence was implemented with five from a batch of 8 which were new to County Bus in 1990 for Route 66 Romford Station to Leytonstone. Seen in High Street during July 2001 working service 3 (normally a midibus allocation). The elegant Town Hall tower is visible in the background. Bottom right: 3406: P326HVX a standard Dennis Dart/Plaxton Pointer as featured in the rival First Eastern National fleet, seen loading on stand 14 in Colchester bus station bound for Dedham (heart of Constable country) on an Essex CC contract journey in February 2003. GR Mills (6)

Fresh Saloon Intake

Leyland Lynxes made a return to Magdalen Street in January 2001 when five former County Bus & Coach examples were transferred from Harlow together with four DAF/Ikarus buses to replace the Volvo single-deckers. In April the open-top Atlantean 55 (Arriva no 5301), which had been withdrawn in September 2000, was transferred to Luton and subsequently used as a promotions/publicity bus. The circular tour of the town was not reintroduced and City Sightseeing stepped in to provide a replacement; initially provided by Ensignbus of Purfleet in 2001/2 and Phoenix, Maldon for 2003 with ex Colchester bus 77!

Service revisions on 21 May 2001 saw service 2 curtailed to run every 15 minutes between Highwoods - St Johns - Town Centre and service 2A every 30 minutes between Highwoods – Eastwood - Ipswich Road - Town Centre - North Station. Service 2B was withdrawn. Service 8A was extended beyond General Hospital to Highwoods, providing a 15 minute frequency combined with service 5.

Weekend Gains

Arriva Colchester gained Essex County Council contracts for the Saturday timetables on services 50/92 between Colchester and Tollesbury. These services, which had been operated by G W Osborne & Sons, were deregistered by Hedingham Omnibuses from 9 June 2001. Further gains from 4 August were the Saturday journeys between Tollesbury and Witham (91) and Tollesbury and Maldon (95). The latter contracts lasted until 30 March 2002 when they were regained by Hedingham, but the Colchester services (50/92) continue to be operated by Arriva from Magdalen Street.

New Control

In a further reorganisation of the Arriva group, control of Colchester (together with Southend and Grays depots) was transferred from Arriva the Shires and Essex, based in Luton, to Arriva Southern Counties at Maidstone on 25 November 2001. Their offices were originally those of Boroline, formerly Maidstone Borough Transport, at Armstrong Road.

Alterations to services introduced on 28 October 2002 included a simplification of the service 1 group but with a reduction in frequency from every 7/8 minutes to every 10 minutes and revised routes in Greenstead. The variants 1B (via Westlands and Longridge) and 1C (via The Commons and Bridgebrook) were withdrawn and replaced by an extended service 3. This Monday to Saturday service ran generally every hour from Hythe (Tesco) via Longridge, Bridgebrook, Harwich Road, town centre, Maldon Road, The Commons, Heath Road, Straight Road, Westlands, Dugard Avenue and Five Ways to a new development at Lakelands in Stanway.

The recently introduced service 194 (Colchester - East Bergholt) was withdrawn after operation on 26 October 2002 and replaced by an extension of First Eastern Counties service 93, thus restoring the through Colchester to Ipswich link, albeit only every two hours.

Further reductions came with the withdrawal of service 133 (Braintree – Stansted Airport) after operation on 5 April 2003. The County Council let a new daily contract for the service to Stansted Transit of Buntingford. As a result the fleet strength reduced to 40 vehicles but a further acquired double-decker was added in September to cover a new works contract hire between Ipswich and a poultry packing factory at Witham.

During the summer of 2003, rumours circulated that Arriva wished to dispose of the Colchester operations in a possible deal with First Group - these rumours were strongly denied in the trade press.

Further Service Changes

Alterations to the bus services introduced on 5 April 2004 involved further reductions. Service 2A between Highwoods and North Station was reduced to hourly between the peak service on Mondays to Fridays and between 0930 and 1730hrs on Saturdays. Service 3 was revised again to run from town centre via Harwich Road, Bridgebrook and Longridge Park to Greenstead roundabout and thence via a clockwise loop around the University of Essex; the Saturday timetable was withdrawn and the section between town centre and Stanway (Lakelands) was replaced by a new service 4 consisting of three off-peak journeys at two-hourly intervals on Mondays to Fridays. Service 5 was rerouted in the northern part of the Highwoods development to serve Gavin Way and Maximus Drive. Also service 1 was rerouted in Greenstead to serve Hickory Avenue (South) again and terminate opposite Elm Crescent before continuing via Forest Road. There were also minor timetable alterations to services 2, 8, 8A and 8B.

One Hundred Years

28 July 2004 marked the 100th anniversary of public transport operated from Colchester's Magdalen Street depot. For Eighty nine years the operation was in municipal hands and today the depot premises remain in the ownership of the local authority leased to the current operators, Arriva.

There have been many changes since the start with sixteen trams in 1904, the introduction of motor buses in 1928 and the fleet strength reaching a peak of 60 buses and coaches in 1988 before reducing to the current level of 39.

Throughout the period the system has expanded to cater for the development of Colchester. There has always been a devoted team of employees who have enjoyed the good times and struggled with the bad times. Nevertheless Colchester's transport undertaking has achieved 100 years even though it is now in private ownership.

ARRIVA COACH INTAKE

4344: HDZ8354 (previously C904JOF/245DOC/C566LOG) a unique coach in the Colchester fleet. The Bova Futura started life with Central, Walsall in 1986; later with County, Harlow in Samsons Cheshunt (as 3079) duo blue and white livery. Top left: In as acquired by Colchester livery of Leaside brown and white as shown arriving at the Leisure Centre in May 1998 driven by Keith Sadler. Top Right: Freshly repainted into Arriva hue seen in Friday Woods, schools activity area, during June 1998.

Centre left: BAZ7384 (ex C210PPE) Leyland Tiger/Plaxton one of a dozen new to LCBS in 1985 as STL10. Back in original home area in this January 2001 view in Hertford. Centre right: 2196: J27UNY Leyland Tiger with Plaxton 321 body to Duple design. Originally one of five new to Bebbs, Llantwit Fadre (subsequent owner of 55; AEC Reliance/Plaxton in 1975) but ex New Enterprise, Tonbridge. Seen freshly repainted and into Colchester service during June 2002.

4352: M52AWW One of a pair of Scania K113/VanHool Alizee became the front-line coaches for the 2002 season, and introduced a chassis and body make not previously featured in the Colchester fleet. Originally operated by the Yorkshire Woollen in National Express AirLink later Flightlink liveries. Finally in Greenline livery for the Southend to London service prior to transfer to Colchester. Seen at North Rail Station working for Great Eastern in March 2002.

GR Mills (5)

Top left: GEV200B a 1964 Ford 400E Van in full CCT bus livery seen during September 1966 in Vineyard Street, with KTD551C Leyland Atlantean/Park Royal at rear Colchester's first ever demonstrator bus D1. After sale the van was bought by long surviving driver, the late Stan Rice.

Top right: 94: Q486MHK then on trade plates 423VW a 1946 Scammell Pioneer 6x4 an ex MoD vehicle painted orange pulls 85-MEV85V Leyland AN68/ECW out of the bus station in to Queen Street, bound for the depot in June 1980.

Centre left: 96: PPU329R Scania 80 prepares to hitch up to 354 JIL 2194 Greenway in the lay-by outside Sir Charles Lucas School on Greenstead Estate, in March 1997.   RR Eves

Centre right: 998: B732XJD a Leyland Freighter 15:43 an ex Arriva London towing truck in LT red with bright yellow V on front prepares to give a route branded Dennis Dart SLF a suspended tow back to Magdalen Street from the lay-by outside Sainsburys at Tollgate in February 1999.

IN TRAINING

93:   ABN771V – 1979 Ford R1114/Plaxton Paramount C53F acquired from Ipswich Travel specifically for driver training in February 1991, as the coach had a manual gearbox and was capable of 50mph so that a trainee could gain an all groups PSV licence. Back on previous 'home' ground caught approaching Stoke Bridge in Ipswich during June 1993. Since Arriva days various Leyland National Greenways and two different Lynx have been based in Colchester for short term training periods; the vehicle normally returning to Southend. 3066/E966 PME Lynx has been the most regular visitor 2002-4.

GR Mills (4)

24: 9667VX
Numerically the town's first Leyland pioneered the first journey into the new Greenstead Estate on 18 June 1961. The shiny bus then only 7 months old is seen in Sycamore Road, with Laburnum Grove in the background. R.R.Eves

SIGNIFICANT SIXTIES

22: 194MNO
A 5 year old AEC Regent V was chosen to be decorated for the Diamond Jubilee of the municipal operations and operated with flags and illuminations for a week. Seen at the Severalls terminus on 4 October 1964 with the late Stan Rice, long serving driver at the wheel.   G.R.Mills

50: AVX50G
A very smart Leyland Atlantean/Massey from the second batch supplied new to Colchester Corporation Transport. All ten were crew operated as this view of the bus emerging from Vineyard Street in March 1969 clearly shows with the conductor aiding safe exit into St John's Street with a cautionary hand signal. The Brewers Arms is visible on the right. R.R.Eves

Colchester Corporation
Transport Department

FREE ISSUE

TIME TABLE
COMMENCING JANUARY 16th, 1933

JOSLINS, LTD.
General and Furnishing Ironmongers
Complete House Furnishers
CARPETS, RUGS, AND LINOLEUMS
CHINA, GLASS AND EARTHENWARE
REGISTERED ELECTRICAL CONTRACTORS
(NATIONAL REGISTER)
WIRELESS EXPERTS
108 & 109 HIGH STREET
COLCHESTER. TELEPHONE 2208
Cullingford & Co., Ltd., Printers, Colchester.

COLCHESTER CORPORATION TRANSPORT
★
Official
TIME TABLE
★
MARCH 4th, 1946
and until further notice
★
Price - ONE PENNY

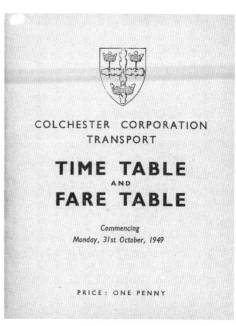

COLCHESTER CORPORATION TRANSPORT
TIME TABLE
AND
FARE TABLE
Commencing
Monday, 31st October, 1949
PRICE: ONE PENNY

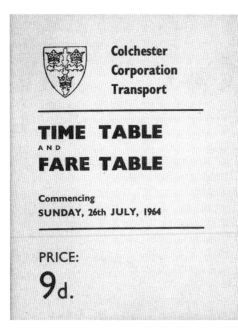

Colchester
Corporation
Transport

TIME TABLE
AND
FARE TABLE
Commencing
SUNDAY, 26th JULY, 1964

PRICE:
9d.

Colchester Borough Transport
CBT
BUS TIMETABLE
Including
ROUTE MAP
Commencing SUNDAY, 30th MARCH, 1975
8p

Bus Guide & Map
From 1 August 1994
Colchester Borough Transport

Guide to
Services and
Route Map
Colchester
bus times
From April 1998
Timetables
for all buses
serving
Colchester
ARRIVA
serving Colchester

LOCAL BUS SERVICES (AS AT 5 APRIL 2004)

COMMERCIAL:

Service	Route	Basic weekday frequency
1/1A	Greenstead, Elm Crescent (1) or Hamlet Drive (1A) - Harwich Road - Town Centre - Maldon Road - Shrub End (1) or Prettygate (1A) - Ambrose Avenue	Mondays to Saturdays every 10 minutes
2	Highwoods - St Johns - Ipswich Road - Town Centre	Mondays to Saturdays every 15 minutes
2A	Highwoods - Eastwood - Ipswich Road - Town Centre - North Station	Mondays to Saturdays off-peak every 60 minutes
3	University of Essex - Greenstead - Longridge Park – Bridgebrook -Harwich Road – Town Centre	Mondays to Fridays every 60 minutes
4	Stanway (Lakelands) - Westlands - Heath Road - Prettygate - Maldon Road - Town Centre	Mondays to Fridays 3 return journeys
5	Highwoods - Mile End - North Station - Town Centre – Lexden - Home Farm - Fiveways - Stanway, Tollgate	Mondays to Saturdays every 30 minutes
8	Monkwick - Mersea Road - Town Centre - North Station - General Hospital - Horkesley Heath	Mondays to Saturdays every 30 minutes
8A	Monkwick - Silver Oyster - Mersea Road - Town Centre - North Station - General Hospital - Highwoods	Mondays to Saturdays every 30 minutes
8B	Town Centre - North Station - General Hospital - Boxted	Mondays to Saturdays 2 peak journeys
9	Town Centre - Harwich Road - Bridgebrook - St Johns - Tyehurst - Highwoods, Gilberd School	Mondays to Fridays one return journey, financially funded by ECC on schooldays

ESSEX COUNTY COUNCIL CONTRACT SERVICES

Service	Route	Basic weekday frequency
1E	Greenstead, Elm Crescent - Harwich Road - Town Centre - Maldon Road - Prettygate - Ambrose Avenue, returns via Shrub End	Mondays to Saturdays evenings every 60 mins
2E	Highwoods - St Johns - Ipswich Road - Town Centre - North Station - Mile End - Highwoods	Mondays to Saturdays evenings every 65 mins
8E	Monkwick - Mersea Road - Town Centre - North Station - General Hospital - Horkesley Heath	Mondays to Saturdays evenings every 65 mins
11	Highwoods - Tyehurst - St Johns - Harwich Road - Cowdray Avenue - North Station	Mondays to Fridays commuter service
15	Shrub End - Prettygate - Home Farm - Lexden - Cymbeline Way - North Station	Mondays to Fridays commuter service
16	Old Heath - Southway - St Helena School	Schooldays, one return journey
16A	Barnhall - Mersea Road - Southway - St Helena School	Schooldays, one return journey
17	West Bergholt - North Station - Stanway School	Schooldays, one return journey
50/92	Tollesbury - Birch (92) or Layer-de-la-Haye and Maypole Green (50) - Colchester	Saturdays, six return journeys
83	Colne Engaine (Mondays) or Mount Bures (Tuesdays) - Chappel Corner - Great Tey - Marks Tey - Stanway - Colchester	Mondays to Saturdays two return journeys
87/87A	Dedham Heath - Dedham - Ardleigh - Parsons Heath - Cowdray Avenue - Colchester	Mondays to Saturdays two journeys
172	Messing – Tiptree – Layer Marney – Easthorpe – Copford – Colchester	Wednesdays, one return journey
247	Colchester – Langham – Dedham Heath – Dedham (extended to East East Bergholt – one afternoon journey schooldays)	Mondays to Saturdays three return journeys

COMPLETE FLEET LIST

PRE-WAR

Fleet No	Reg No	Chassis	Body Builder	Seating	Date In	Date Out	
1	VW 4389	Dennis G	Strachan & Brown	B20F	5/28	3/44	New
2	VW 4390	Dennis G	Strachan & Brown	B20F	5/28	12/44	New
3	VW 4391	Dennis G	Strachan & Brown	B20F	5/28	9/45	New
4	VW 4392	Dennis G	Strachan & Brown	B20F	5/28	12/43	New
5	VW 5125	Dennis E	Strachan & Brown	B32D	6/28	7/42	New
6	VW 5126	Dennis E	Strachan & Brown	B32D	6/28	12/40	New
7	VW 6463	Dennis E	Strachan & Brown	B32D	9/28	6/42	New
8	VW 6462	Dennis E	Strachan & Brown	B32D	9/28	7/43	New
9	VW 6464	Dennis E	Strachan & Brown	B32D	9/28	10/43	New
10	VW 6482	Dennis H	Strachan & Brown	O24/24R	9/28	8/39	New
11	VW 6481	Dennis H	Strachan & Brown	O24/24R	9/28	11/43	New
12	VW 8425	Dennis H	Strachan & Brown	O24/24R	2/29	12/43	New
13	VW 8426	Dennis E	Strachan & Brown	B32D	2/29	6/39	New
14	VW 8424	Dennis H	Strachan & Brown	H24/24R	2/29	12/43	New
15	VX 3223	Dennis HS	Strachan & Brown	H24/24R	12/29	5/44	New
16	VX 3224	Dennis HS	Strachan & Brown	H24/24R	12/29	6/45	New
17	VX 3222	Dennis HS	Strachan & Brown	H24/24R	12/29	12/43	New
18	VX 2746	Dennis EV	Strachan & Brown	B32D	10/29	8/45	New
19	VX 2745	Dennis EV	Strachan & Brown	B32D	10/29	8/45	New
20	VX 5551	AEC Regent	Short	H24/24R	5/30	4/49	New
21	VX 5552	AEC Regent	Short	H24/24R	5/30	12/48	New
22	VX 5553	AEC Regent	Short	H24/24R	5/30	4/49	New
23	VX 5554	AEC Regal	Willet	B32D	5/30	3/47	New
24	EV 3599	AEC Regal	Willet	B32D	11/31	4/47	New
25	EV 3600	AEC Regent	Ransomes	H24/24R	11/31	2/49	New
26	EV 3601	AEC Regent	Ransomes	H24/24R	11/31	2/49	New
27	DPU 416	AEC Regent	Strachan	H24/24R	7/36	4/49	New
28	DPU 417	AEC Regent	Strachan	H24/24R	7/36	11/52	New
29	DPU 418	AEC Regent	Strachan	H24/24R	7/36	11/52	New
30	GVW 946	AEC Regent	Massey	H26/26R	3/39	5/57	New
31	GVW 947	AEC Regent	Massey	H26/26R	3/39	5/57	New
32	GVW 948	AEC Regent	Massey	H26/26R	3/39	5/57	New
33	GVW 949	AEC Regent	Massey	H26/26R	3/39	8/56	New
34	GVW 950	AEC Regent	Massey	H26/26R	3/39	6/57	New

NOTES:

1 - 4 were reduced to B18F in 1935
5 - 9 were reduced to B31D in 1937
10 - 12 were converted to H24/24R in 1930
10/11 were converted to H26/22R and 12 converted to H26/26R in 1936
13/18/19/23/24 were reduced to B31D in 1937

WARTIME UTILITY STOCK

Fleet No	Reg No	Chassis	Body Builder	Seating	Date In	Date Out	
35	JPU 581	Bristol K5G	Bristol	H30/26R	6/42	8/56	New
36	JPU 582	Bristol K5G	Bristol	H30/26R	6/42	7/56	New
37	JTW 749	Guy Arab I 5LW	Park Royal	H30/26R	5/43	1/59	New
38	JTW 750	Guy Arab I 5LW	Park Royal	H30/26R	5/43	1/59	New
39	JTW 982	Guy Arab II 5LW	Weymann	H30/26R	10/43	3/61	New
40	JTW 983	Guy Arab II 5LW	Weymann	H30/26R	10/43	1/59	New
41	JVW 579	Guy Arab II 5LW	Strachan	H30/26R	4/44	12/60	New
42	JVW 580	Guy Arab II 5LW	Strachan	H30/26R	5/44	11/60	New
43	JVW 581	Guy Arab II 5LW	Strachan	H30/26R	5/44	9/62	New
44	JVW 582	Guy Arab II 5LW	Strachan	H30/26R	7/44	12/60	New
45	JVW 242	Guy Arab II 5LW	Park Royal	H30/26R	11/43	8/56	New
46	KEV 331	Bristol K6A	Duple	H30/26R	8/45	6/64	New
47	KEV 624	Bristol K6A	Park Royal	H30/26R	9/45	7/64	New
48	KEV 625	Bristol K6A	Duple	H30/26R	9/45	1/63	New
49	KEV 738	Bristol K6A	Park Royal	H30/26R	11/45	1/63	New
50	KEV 804	Bristol K6A	Park Royal	H30/26R	11/45	2/63	New

POST-WAR

Fleet No	Reg No	Chassis	Body Builder	Seating	Date In	Date Out	
51	KPU 515	AEC Regent II	Massey	H30/26R	4/47	2/66	New
52	KPU 516	AEC Regent II	Massey	H30/26R	4/47	1/66	New
53	KPU 517	AEC Regent II	Massey	H30/26R	3/47	6/64	New
54	KPU 518	AEC Regent II	Massey	H30/26R	3/47	2/66	New
55	KPU 519	Crossley DD42/3T	Massey	H30/26R	11/48	9/67	New
1	OHK 429	Daimler CVD6	Roberts	H30/26R	3/49	2/66	New
2	OHK 430	Daimler CVD6	Roberts	H30/26R	3/49	1/66	New
3	OHK 431	Daimler CVD6	Roberts	H30/26R	4/49	9/68	New
4	OHK 432	Daimler CVD6	Roberts	H30/26R	4/49	9/68	New
5	OHK 433	Daimler CVD6	Roberts	H30/26R	4/49	7/68	New
6	SVW 451	Crossley DD42/7	Crossley	H30/26R	6/51	1/68	New
7	SVW 452	Crossley DD42/7	Crossley	H30/26R	7/51	5/68	New
8	TVX 496	Crossley DD42/7	Crossley	H30/26R	10/52	6/68	New
9	TVX 497	Crossley DD42/7	Crossley	H30/26R	10/52	3/68	New
10	WPU 732	AEC Regent III	Massey	H30/26R	9/53	1/71	New
11	WPU 733	AEC Regent III	Massey	H30/26R	9/53	5/71	New
12	WPU 734	AEC Regent III	Massey	H30/26R	9/53	3/71	New
13	679 HEV	AEC Regent V	Massey	H33/28R	9/56	8/71	New
14	680 HEV	AEC Regent V	Massey	H33/28R	8/56	5/71	New
15	681 HEV	AEC Regent V	Massey	H33/28R	8/56	11/75	New
16	682 HEV	AEC Regent V	Massey	H33/28R	9/56	9/76	New
17	1295 F	AEC Regent V	Massey	H33/28R	6/57	4/73	New
18	1296 F	AEC Regent V	Massey	H33/28R	5/57	12/72	New
19	1297 F	AEC Regent V	Massey	H33/28R	5/57	4/73	New
20	1298 F	AEC Regent V	Massey	H33/28R	5/57	5/73	New
21	193 MNO	AEC Regent V	Massey	H33/28R	2/59	12/73	New
22	194 MNO	AEC Regent V	Massey	H33/28R	2/59	12/73	New
23	195 MNO	AEC Regent V	Massey	H33/28R	2/59	7/71	New

In order to clear a block of 15 consecutive numbers for the Bristol RELLs several AEC Regent Vs were renumbered: 15 to 55 and later to 5; 16 to 23, later 60 and finally 2; 17 to 13; 21 to 63; and 22 to 62

LEYLAND ERA

24	9667 VX	Leyland Titan PD2/31	Massey	H33/28R	11/60	12/71	New
25	9668 VX	Leyland Titan PD2/31	Massey	H33/28R	11/60	12/71	New
26	9669 VX	Leyland Titan PD2/31	Massey	H33/28R	12/60	12/71	New
27	9670 VX	Leyland Titan PD2/31	Massey	H33/28R	12/60	12/71	New
28	9671 VX	Leyland Titan PD2/31	Massey	H33/28R	1/61	12/71	New
29	MWC 129	Leyland Titan PD2A/31	Massey	H33/28R	1/63	5/77	New
30	MWC 130	Leyland Titan PD2A/31	Massey	H33/28R	3/63	5/77	New
31	MWC 131	Leyland Titan PD2A/31	Massey	H33/28R	3/63	5/77	New
32	MWC 132	Leyland Titan PD2A/31	Massey	H33/28R	3/63	5/77	New
33	MWC 133	Leyland Titan PD2A/31	Massey	H33/28R	2/63	5/77	New
34	MWC 134	Leyland Titan PD2A/31	Massey	H33/28R	2/63	5/77	New
35	MWC 135	Leyland Titan PD2A/31	Massey	H33/28R	3/63	6/76	New
36	CWC 36B	Leyland Titan PD2A/30 Spl	Massey	H33/28R	6/64	5/77	New
37	CWC 37B	Leyland Titan PD2A/30 Spl	Massey	H33/28R	7/64	5/77	New
38	CWC 38B	Leyland Titan PD2A/30 Spl	Massey	H33/28R	7/64	5/77	New
39	OVX 139D	Leyland Titan PD2A/30	Massey	H33/28R	3/66	5/78	New
40	OVX 140D	Leyland Titan PD2A/30	Massey	H33/28R	2/66	12/79	New
41	OVX 141D	Leyland Titan PD2A/30	Massey	H33/28R	3/66	6/78	New
42	OVX 142D	Leyland Titan PD2A/30	Massey	H33/28R	2/66	12/79	New
43	OVX 143D	Leyland Titan PD2A/30	Massey	H33/28R	2/66	6/78	New
44	OVX 144D	Leyland Titan PD2A/30	Massey	H33/28R	2/66	1/80	New
45	WEV 745F	Leyland Atlantean PDR1/1	Massey	H43/31F	12/67	10/80	New
46	WEV 746F	Leyland Atlantean PDR1/1	Massey	H43/31F	12/67	8/80	New
47	WEV 747F	Leyland Atlantean PDR1/1	Massey	H43/31F	12/67	10/80	New
48	YWC 648F	Leyland Atlantean PDR1/1	Massey	H43/31F	6/68	10/88	New
49	YWC 649F	Leyland Atlantean PDR1/1	Massey	H43/31F	6/68	3/86	New
50	AVX 50G	Leyland Atlantean PDR1/1	Massey	H43/31F	9/68	8/85	New
51	AVX 51G	Leyland Atlantean PDR1/1	Massey	H43/31F	9/68	10/80	New
52	AVX 52G	Leyland Atlantean PDR1/1	Massey	H43/31F	9/68	2/80	New
53	AVX 53G	Leyland Atlantean PDR1/1	Massey	H43/31F	10/68	10/80	New
54	AVX 54G	Leyland Atlantean PDR1/1	Massey	H43/31F	10/68	12/80	New

NOTES:
39-44 Platform Doors fitted by Southfields Coachworks Loughborough 1970/71
48 was converted to O43/31F in 8/79
36 was renumbered 96 in 6/78 as training vehicle
46 was renumbered 96 in 4/81 as training vehicle

SECOND-HAND AND SINGLE DECKER ERA DAWNS

Fleet No	Reg No	Chassis	Body Builder	Seating	Date New	Date In	Date Out	Ex:-
55	652 GVA	AEC Reliance	Plaxton	B55F	8/63	6/70	3/75	Hedingham (L53)
1	TRJ 109	AEC Reliance	Weymann	B45F	2/62	2/71	5/76	SELNEC (71)
2	TRJ 102	AEC Reliance	Weymann	B45F	2/62	2/71	8/73	SELNEC (65)
3	TRJ 103	AEC Reliance	Weymann	B45F	2/62	2/71	8/73	SELNEC (66)
4	TRJ 104	AEC Reliance	Weymann	B45F	2/62	2/71	3/75	SELNEC (67)
5	TRJ 105	AEC Reliance	Weymann	B45F	2/62	2/71	11/74	SELNEC (68)
6	TRJ 106	AEC Reliance	Weymann	B45F	2/62	2/71	5/76	SELNEC (69)
7	197 GJF	AEC Reliance	Marshall	B53F	12/63	10/71	3/75	Leicester (197)
8	198 GJF	AEC Reliance	Marshall	B53F	12/63	10/71	3/75	Leicester (198)
9	ABC 195B	AEC Reliance	Marshall	B53F	3/64	10/71	6/76	Leicester (195)
10	ABC 196B	AEC Reliance	Marshall	B53F	3/64	10/71	5/76	Leicester (196)
11	GBC 199D	AEC Reliance	Marshall	B53F	5/66	10/71	6/76	Leicester (199)
24	SWC 24K	Bristol RELL6L	ECW	B53F	5/72	5/72	6/87	New
25	SWC 25K	Bristol RELL6L	ECW	B53F	5/72	5/72	2/88	New
26	SWC 26K	Bristol RELL6L	ECW	B53F	5/72	5/72	3/88	New
27	SWC 27K	Bristol RELL6L	ECW	B53F	5/72	5/72	6/84	New
28	SWC 28K	Bristol RELL6L	ECW	B53F	5/72	5/72	6/87	New
14	YWC 14L	Bristol RELL6L	ECW	B53F	4/73	4/73	4/81	New
15	YWC 15L	Bristol RELL6L	ECW	B53F	4/73	4/73	4/81	New
16	YWC 16L	Bristol RELL6L	ECW	B53F	5/73	5/73	8/88	New
17	YWC 17L	Bristol RELL6L	ECW	B53F	5/73	5/73	5/81	New
18	YWC 18L	Bristol RELL6L	ECW	B53F	5/73	5/73	3/88	New
19	OWC 719M	Bristol RELL6L	ECW	B53F	12/73	12/73	9/87	New
20	OWC 720M	Bristol RELL6L	ECW	B53F	12/73	12/73	1/88	New
21	OWC 721M	Bristol RELL6L	ECW	B53F	12/73	12/73	11/87	New
22	OWC 722M	Bristol RELL6L	ECW	B53F	12/73	12/73	8/88	New
23	OWC 723M	Bristol RELL6L	ECW	B53F	12/73	12/73	4/88	New

Notes:
55 (652 GVA) was renumbered 12 in 11/71

STANDARDISATION

Fleet No	Reg No	Chassis	Body Builder	Seating	Date In	Date Out	Ex:-
55	JHK 495N	Leyland Atlantean AN68/1R	ECW	H43/31F	4/75	4/01	New
56	JHK 496N	Leyland Atlantean AN68/1R	ECW	H43/31F	4/75	9/89	New
57	JHK 497N	Leyland Atlantean AN68/1R	ECW	H43/31F	4/75	1/89	New
58	JHK 498N	Leyland Atlantean AN68/1R	ECW	H43/31F	4/75	9/89	New
59	JHK 499N	Leyland Atlantean AN68/1R	ECW	H43/31F	4/75	6/89	New
60	JHK 500N	Leyland Atlantean AN68/1R	ECW	H43/31F	4/75	1/89	New
61	NNO 61P	Leyland Atlantean AN68A/1R	ECW	H43/31F	5/76	8/91	New
62	NNO 62P	Leyland Atlantean AN68A/1R	ECW	H43/31F	5/76	2/91	New
63	NNO 63P	Leyland Atlantean AN68A/1R	ECW	H43/31F	5/76	10/91	New
64	NNO 64P	Leyland Atlantean AN68A/1R	ECW	H43/31F	6/76	1/91	New
65	NNO 65P	Leyland Atlantean AN68A/1R	ECW	H43/31F	5/76	10/92	New
66	NNO 66P	Leyland Atlantean AN68A/1R	ECW	H43/31F	5/76	3/91	New
67	TPU 67R	Leyland Atlantean AN68A/1R	ECW	H43/31F	5/77	12/97	New
68	TPU 68R	Leyland Atlantean AN68A/1R	ECW	H43/31F	5/77	8/98	New
69	TPU 69R	Leyland Atlantean AN68A/1R	ECW	H43/31F	5/77	7/98	New
70	TPU 70R	Leyland Atlantean AN68A/1R	ECW	H43/31F	5/77	10/92	New
71	TPU 71R	Leyland Atlantean AN68A/1R	ECW	H43/31F	5/77	9/98	New
72	TPU 72R	Leyland Atlantean AN68A/1R	ECW	H43/31F	5/77	10/92	New
73	TPU 73R	Leyland Atlantean AN68A/1R	ECW	H43/31F	5/77	2/97	New
74	TPU 74R	Leyland Atlantean AN68A/1R	ECW	H43/31F	5/77	5/98	New
75	TPU 75R	Leyland Atlantean AN68A/1R	ECW	H43/31F	6/77	9/98	New
76	TPU 76R	Leyland Atlantean AN68A/1R	ECW	H43/31F	6/77	5/98	New
77	YNO 77S	Leyland Atlantean AN68A/1R	ECW	H43/31F	6/78	11/98	New
78	YNO 78S	Leyland Atlantean AN68A/1R	ECW	H43/31F	6/78	12/98	New
79	YNO 79S	Leyland Atlantean AN68A/1R	ECW	H43/31F	6/78	8/95	New
80	YNO 80S	Leyland Atlantean AN68A/1R	ECW	H43/31F	6/78	2/99	New
81	YNO 81S	Leyland Atlantean AN68A/1R	ECW	H43/31F	6/78	2/99	New
82	YNO 82S	Leyland Atlantean AN68A/1R	ECW	H43/31F	6/78	4/99	New
101	DHK 101T	Leyland Leopard PSU3E/4R	Duple	C51F	2/79	1/94	New
102	DHK 102T	Leyland Leopard PSU3E/4R	Duple	C51F	2/79	2/94	New
83	MEV 83V	Leyland Atlantean AN68A/1R	ECW	H43/31F	12/79	1/99	New
84	MEV 84V	Leyland Atlantean AN68A/1R	ECW	H43/31F	12/79	2/99	New
85	MEV 85V	Leyland Atlantean AN68A1R	ECW	H43/31F	12/79	12/99	New
86	MEV 86V	Leyland Atlantean AN68A/1R	ECW	H43/31F	12/79	7/99	New
87	MEV 87V	Leyland Atlantean AN68A/1R	ECW	H43/31F	12/79	10/99	New
88	RVW 88W	Leyland Atlantean AN68A/1R	ECW	H43/31F	8/80	8/99	New
89	RVW 89W	Leyland Atlantean AN68A/1R	ECW	H43/31F	8/80	12/99	New
90	RVW 90W	Leyland Atlantean AN68A/1R	ECW	H43/31F	8/80	12/99	New

NOTES:
55 (JHK 495N) was converted to O43/31F in 6/89, renumbered 95 in 9/97 and to 5301 with Arriva in 1/99
68, 71/5/7/8, 80-90 were renumbered 5303/5-8/10-20 with Arriva in 1/99
69 passed to C-Line, Macclesfield, Midland Red North, Cannock and BeeLine Buzz, Manchester from 10/92 returning "home" in 8/94

BOROUGH TRANSPORT... LAST ORDERS

Fleet No	Reg No	Chassis	Body	Seating	Date New	Date In	Date Out	Ex:-
51	MVK 538R	Leyland Atlantean AN68A/2R	Alexander	H48/34F	12/76	12/83	10/90	Tyne & Wear (538)
52	MVK 546R	Leyland Atlantean AN68A/2R	Alexander	H48/34F	1/77	9/84	3/90	Tyne & Wear (546)
53	MVK 548R	Leyland Atlantean AN68A/2R	Alexander	H48/34F	1/77	9/84	3/90	Tyne & Wear (548)
41	C41 HHJ	Leyland Olympian ONLXCT/1R	ECW	H47/31F	10/85	10/85		New
42	C42 HHJ	Leyland Olympian ONLXCT/1RH	ECW	H47/31F	10/85	10/85	1/94	New
43	D43 RWC	Leyland Olympian ONLXCT/1RH	ECW	H47/31F	9/86	9/86	7/02	New
44	D44 RWC	Leyland Olympian ONLXCT/1RH	ECW	H47/31F	9/86	9/86	1/94	New
31	D31 RWC	Leyland Lynx LX112TL11FR1	Leyland	B49F	10/86	10/86	2/94	New
32	D32 RWC	Leyland Lynx LX112TL11FR1	Leyland	B49F	10/86	10/86	3/94	New
103	OHE 274X	Leyland Tiger TRCTL11/3R	Duple	C53F	6/82	5/87	7/00	West Riding (274)
104	OHE 280X	Leyland Tiger TRCTL11/3R	Duple	C53F	6/82	5/87	10/00	West Riding (280)
54	XJA 517L	Leyland Atlantean AN68/1R	Park Royal	H43/32F	11/72	12/87	7/89	GM Buses (7126)
33	E33 EVW	Leyland Lynx LX112L10ZR1	Leyland	B49F	1/88	1/88	4/94	New
34	E34 EVW	Leyland Lynx LX112L10ZR1	Leyland	B49F	1/88	1/88	4/94	New
35	E35 EVW	Leyland Lynx LX112L10ZR1	Leyland	B49F	2/88	2/88	4/94	New
36	E36 EVW	Leyland Lynx LX112L10ZR1	Leyland	B49F	2/88	2/88	4/94	New
37	E37 EVW	Leyland Lynx LX112L10ZR1	Leyland	B49F	2/88	2/88	4/94	New
45	F245 MTW	Leyland Olympian ONCL10/1RZ	Leyland	H43/29F	9/88	9/88		New
46	F246 MTW	Leyland Olympian ONCL10/1RZ	Leyland	H43/29F	9/88	9/88		New
11	F111 NPU	MCW Metrorider MF158/013	MCW	DP29F	11/88	11/88	2/91	New
12	F112 NPU	MCW Metrorider MF158/014	MCW	B31F	11/88	11/88	2/91	New
13	F113 NPU	MCW Metrorider MF158/014	MCW	B31F	11/88	11/88	2/91	New
14	F114 NPU	MCW Metrorider MF158/014	MCW	B31F	11/88	11/88	2/91	New
15	F115 NPU	MCW Metrorider MF158/014	MCW	B31F	11/88	11/88	2/91	New
38	G38 YHJ	Leyland Lynx LX2R11C15Z4R	Leyland	B49F	11/89	11/89	4/94	New
39	G39 YHJ	Leyland Lynx LX2R11C15Z4R	Leyland	B49F	11/89	11/89	4/94	New
40	G40 YHJ	Leyland Lynx LX2R11C15Z4R	Leyland	B49F	11/89	11/89	8/94	New
105	G105 AVX	Dennis Javelin	Duple	C53FT	1/90	1/90	11/93	New
106	G106 AVX	Dennis Javelin	Duple	C52FT	1/90	1/90	11/93	New
107	H107 JAR	Volvo B10M-60	Ikarus	C49FT	10/90	10/90	11/93	New
108	H108 JAR	Volvo B10M-60	Ikarus	C48FT	10/90	10/90	11/93	New
30	H130 LPU	Leyland Lynx LX2R11C15Z4	Leyland	B49F	12/90	12/90	8/94	New
28	H28 MJN	Leyland Lynx LX2R11G15Z4R	Leyland	B49F	2/91	2/91	10/94	New
29	H29 MJN	Leyland Lynx LX2R11G15Z4R	Leyland	B49F	2/91	2/91	10/94	New
47	H47 MJN	Leyland Olympian ON2R50C13Z4	Leyland	H43/29F	3/91	3/91		New
48	H48 MJN	Leyland Olympian ON2R50C13Z4	Leyland	H47/31F	3/91	3/91		New
49	H49 MJN	Leyland Olympian ON2R50C13Z4	Leyland	H47/31F	3/91	3/91		New
109	J109 WVW	Leyland Tiger TR2R6ZC21Z68	Plaxton	C53F	8/91	8/91	11/93	New
27	K27 EWC	Leyland Lynx LX2R11C15Z4R	Leyland	B49F	9/92	9/92	8/94	New

NOTES:
41/3/5/6-9 were renumbered 5389/90/7/8, 5407-5409 with Arriva in 1/99
103/4 were renumbered 4302/3 with Arriva in 1/99
45 - 47 were fitted with semi-coach seating
46 was transferred to Southend 2/94 to 8/96
47 was transferred to Southend 12/93 to 8/96

Below Right: 90: RVW90W Most types of CCT/CBT bus since the Guy utility in 1960 has had a farewell tour organised by Geoff Mills and Nicolas Collins. The last such was *very* well attended and shows the four stalwarts who also took part in the Guy trip 40 years earlier. Left to right: Ralph Eves, Geoff Mills, Nicolas Collins and Colin Mills seen at Colchester Zoo in December 1999.

ENDS OF ERAS

Above left: The last day that four AEC Regent V were available for service 30 December 1973. Of the eleven placed in service 1956-9, only two of the 1956 and two of the 1959 deliveries remained. 15/16 (then 55/60) 681-2 HEV pose up on Sheepen Road car/lorry park with 21/2 (then 63/62) 193/4 MNO for the cameras of the local PSV Circle members. GR Mills(2)

LAST COLCHESTER LIVERIED STOCK

Fleet No	Reg No	Chassis	Body	Seating	Date New	Date In	Date Out	Ex:-
9	BVP 809V	Leyland National 2 NL116L11/1R	Leyland	B49F	1/80	6/94	10/97	Midland Fox (3809)
10	BVP 810V	Leyland National 2 NL116L11/1R	Leyland	B49F	2/80	6/94	10/97	Midland Fox (3810)
12	BVP 812V	Leyland National 2 NL116L11/1R	Leyland	B49F	1/80	6/94	10/97	Midland Fox (3812)
19	EON 829V	Leyland National 2 NL116L11/1R	Leyland	B49F	5/80	1/94	12/97	Midland Fox(3829)
21	BVP 821V	Leyland National 2 NL116L11/1R	Leyland	B49F	4/80	1/94	12/97	Midland Fox (3821)
25	EON 825V	Leyland National 2 NL116L11/1R	Leyland	B49F	6/80	6/94	10/97	Midland Fox (3825)
26	EON 826V	Leyland National 2 NL116L11/1R	Leyland	B49F	9/80	1/94	10/97	Midland Fox (3826)
64	PUF 131M	Leyland Atlantean AN68A/1R	Park Royal	H43/30F	5/74	9/94	1/97	London & Country (AN131)
65	MUA 865P	Leyland Atlantean AN68A/1R	Roe	H43/30F	1/76	9/94	2/97	London & Country (AN865)
66	RFR 416P	Leyland Atlantean AN68A/1R	ECW	H43/31F	5/76	9/94	11/96	London & Country (AN416)
70	RFR 421P	Leyland Atlantean AN68A/1R	ECW	H43/31F	5/76	9/94	11/96	London & Country (AN421)
72	RFR 419P	Leyland Atlantean AN68A/1R	ECW	H43/31F	5/76	9/94	9/96	London & Country (AN419)
63	RFR 415P	Leyland Atlantean AN68A/1R	ECW	H43/31F	5/76	3/95	9/96	London & Country (AN415)
62	RCN 96N	Leyland Atlantean AN68/1R	Park Royal	H43/30F	7/74	8/95	9/96	London & Country (AN354)
100	A250 SVW	Leyland Tiger TRCTL11/3R	Duple	C57F	7/85	5/95	3/02	Southend (550)
123	H123 WFM	Mercedes 814D	North West	C24F	4/91	5/96	5/00	Guildford/W Surrey(MC123)
463	NWO 463R	Leyland National 11351A/1R/SC	Leyland Nat	DP48F	3/77	1/96	10/99	London & Country(LNC463)
347	NIW 6507	Leyland National 1151/1R/2402	East Lancs	B49F	3/74	9/96	3/99	London & Country (347)
348	NIW 6508	Leyland National 11351/1R	East Lancs	B49F	10/74	9/96	9/00	London & Country (348)
349	NIW 6509	Leyland National 11351A/1R	East Lancs	B49F	7/77	9/96	1/02	London & Country (349)
350	NIW 6510	Leyland National 2 NL116AL11/2R	East Lancs	B49F	1/82	9/96	10/00	London & Country (350)
351	NIW 6511	Leyland National 11351/1R	East Lancs	B49F	1/76	9/96	11/99	London & Country (351)
352	NIW 6512	Leyland National 2 NL116AL11/2R	East Lancs	B49F	1/82	9/96	3/01	London & Country (352)
354	JIL 2194	Leyland National 11351A/1R	East Lancs	B49F	9/77	9/96	9/00	London & Country (354)
355	JIL 2195	Leyland National 11351/1R	East Lancs	B49F	11/75	9/96	3/01	London & Country (355)
185	XPG 185T	Leyland Atlantean AN68A/1R	Roe	H43/30F	2/79	2/96	9/96	London & Country (AN185)
352	PCN 892M	Leyland Atlantean AN68/1R	Park Royal	H45/31F	7/74	2/96	5/96	London & Country (AN352)
55	A855 VYM	Volvo B10M-61	East Lancs	B49F	5/84	9/97	1/01	County (VEL855)
56	A856 VYM	Volvo B10M-61	East Lancs	B49F	5/84	11/97	1/01	County (VEL856)
57	B857 XYR	Volvo B10M-61	East Lancs	B49F	4/85	8/97	5/02	County (VEL857)
58	B858 XYR	Volvo B10M-61	East Lancs	B49F	5/85	8/97	5/02	County (VEL858)
59	B859 XYR	Volvo B10M-61	East Lancs	B49F	4/85	11/97	5/02	County (VEL859)
60	B860 XYR	Volvo B10M-61	East Lancs	B49F	5/85	9/97	5/02	County (VEL860)
61	B861 XYR	Volvo B10M-61	East Lancs	B49F	5/85	9/97	5/01	County (VEL861)

NOTES:

100 renumbered to 4310, 123 to 2326, 463 to 3303, 347-52/4/5 to 3307-12/04/5, 55-61 to 3315-21 with Arriva in 1/99
55-61 originally had Plaxton C49FT bodies and were rebodied by Grey-Green, London N16 in 3/92 (55/7-60) or 4/92 (56, 61)
347-355 (NIW6507-12, JIL2194/5) were previously registered NEL 863M, GUA 821N, TEL 491R, FCA 8X, LPR 938P, FCA 6X, CBV 779S, JOX 477P

Bottom left: 8: TVX496 all Crossley; 3: OHK431 Daimler/Roberts; 12: WPU734 AEC Regent III/Massey Representing the last three exposed radiator types delivered to Colchester CT. Grouped together beside number 2 garage (left) on land that now forms the open parking area, i.e. after acquisition of property on right.

Bottom right: 31: D31RWC The first Colchester municipal bus to be used in a commercial vehicle exhibition was the first Leyland Lynx delivered. Seen on the Leyland stand at the NEC, Birmingham in October 1986. The lower skirt panel was later painted red within two years of service in the town.   GR Mills(2)

THE ARRIVA ERA DAWNS

Fleet No	Reg No	Chassis	Body	Seating	Date New	Date In	Date Out	Ex:-
336	EYE 336V	MCW Metrobus DR101/12	MCW	H43/28F	7/80	11/97	3/02	Leaside (M336)
220	BYX 220V	MCW Metrobus DR101/12	MCW	H43/28F	5/80	3/98	4/02	Leaside (M220)
299	BYX 299V	MCW Metrobus DR101/12	MCW	H43/28F	5/80	3/99	4/02	Arriva London South (M299)
301	BYX 301V	MCW Metrobus DR101/12	MCW	H43/28F	6/80	2/99	11/02	Arriva London South (M301)
101	BAZ 7384	Leyland Tiger TRCTL11/3RH	Plaxton	C49FT	8/85	4/98		Arriva E Herts & Essex (STL10)
102	HDZ 8354	Bova FHD12-280	Bova	C49FT	3/86	4/98	3/02	Arriva E Herts & Essex (BOV594)
419	P419 HVX	Dennis Dart SLF	Plaxton	B43F	11/96	7/98	7/03	Arriva E Herts & Essex (SLF419)
420	P420 HVX	Dennis Dart SLF	Plaxton	B43F	11/96	7/98	6/03	Arriva E Herts & Essex (SLF420)
422	P422 HVX	Dennis Dart SLF	Plaxton	B43F	11/96	7/98	8/03	Arriva E Herts & Essex (SLF422)
430	P430 HVX	Dennis Dart SLF	Plaxton	B43F	11/96	6/98	6/03	Arriva E Herts & Essex (SLF430)
5364	BYX 283V	MCW Metrobus DR101/12	MCW	H43/28F	5/80	2/99	3/02	Arriva London South (M283)
5365	BYX 263V	MCW Metrobus DR101/12	MCW	H43/28F	6/80	3/99	7/02	Arriva London South (M263)
5350	GYE 410W	MCW Metrobus DR101/12	MCW	H43/28F	10/80	3/99	4/02	Arriva London South (M410)
5259	B289 WUL	MCW Metrobus DR101/17	MCW	H43/28F	6/85	6/99	10/01	Arriva London North (M1289)
5377	TPD 107X	Leyland Olympian ONTL11/1R	Roe	H43/29F	4/82	6/99	5/01	Arriva East Herts & Essex (5377)
3324	E564 BNK	Volvo B10M-56	Plaxton	B54F	2/88	11/99	1/01	Arriva East Herts & Essex (3324)
3325	E565 BNK	Volvo B10M-56	Plaxton	B54F	2/88	11/99	5/01	Arriva East Herts & Essex (3325)
3335	H350 PNO	Leyland Swift LBM6T/2RA	Wadham Stringer	B39F	5/91	12/99	10/00	Arriva East Herts & Essex (3335)
4312	B100 XTW	Leyland Tiger TRCTL11/3RP	Duple	C57F	8/84	11/99	6/02	Arriva Southend (4312)
2058	H408 FGS	Mercedes 811D	Reebur	B31F	12/90	1/00	4/00	Arriva The Shires (2058)
5030	CBD 904T	Bristol VRT/SL3/6LXB	ECW	H43/31F	11/78	2/00	2/00	Arriva The Shires (5030)
3079	F151 KGS	Volvo B10M-56	Plaxton	B54F	10/88	8/00	1/01	Arriva The Shires (3079)
3081	F153 KGS	Volvo B10M-56	Plaxton	B54F	10/88	8/00	7/01	Arriva The Shires (3081)
2383	R953 VPU	Mercedes 0810D	Plaxton	B27F	5/98	8/00	4/04	Arriva Southend (2383)
2384	R954 VPU	Mercedes 0810D	Plaxton	B27F	5/98	8/00	7/02	Arriva Southend (2384)
2369	P939 HVX	Mercedes 711D	Plaxton	B25F	4/97	7/00	4/02	Arriva East Herts & Essex (2369)
2243	R763 DUB	Mercedes 0810D	Plaxton	B27F	9/97	7/00		Arriva East Herts & Essex (2243)
5380	TPD 110X	Leyland Olympian ONTL11/1R	Roe	H43/29F	4/82	10/00	5/01	Arriva East Herts & Essex (5380)
5383	TPD 123X	Leyland Olympian ONTL11/1R	Roe	H43/29F	6/82	4/00	6/01	Arriva East Herts & Essex (5383)
2128	N908 ETM	Mercedes 709D	Plaxton	B27F	9/95	1/01	7/01	Arriva The Shires (2128)
2131	N911 ETM	Mercedes 709D	Plaxton	B27F	9/95	1/01	2/01	Arriva The Shires (2128)
2134	N914 ETM	Mercedes 709D	Plaxton	B27F	9/95	1/01	7/01	Arriva The Shires (2134)
2136	N916 ETM	Mercedes 709D	Plaxton	B27F	9/95	1/01	7/01	Arriva The Shires (2136)
2174	R174 VBM	Mercedes O810D	Plaxton	B27F	8/97	5/01		Arriva The Shires (2174)
2382	R952 VPU	Mercedes O810D	Plaxton	B27F	5/98	5/01		Arriva East Herts & Essex (2382)
2320	L614 FVX	Mercedes 811D	Dormobile	B31F	9/93	1/01	2/02	Arriva East Herts & Essex (2320)
3341	H251 GEV	Leyland Lynx LX2R11C15Z4S	Leyland	B49F	8/90	1/01		Arriva East Herts & Essex (3341)
3342	H252 GEV	Leyland Lynx LX2R11C15Z4S	Leyland	B49F	8/90	1/01		Arriva East Herts & Essex (3342)
3343	H253 GEV	Leyland Lynx LX2R11C15Z4S	Leyland	B49F	8/90	1/01		Arriva East Herts & Essex (3343)
3346	H256 GEV	Leyland Lynx LX2R11C15Z4S	Leyland	B49F	8/90	1/01		Arriva East Herts & Essex (3346)
3347	H257 GEV	Leyland Lynx LX2R11C15Z4S	Leyland	B49F	8/90	1/01		Arriva East Herts & Essex (3347)
3241	M841 DDS	Volvo B6-50	Alexander	B37F	8/94	10/01		Arriva The Shires (3241)
3245	M845 DDS	Volvo B6-50	Alexander	B40F	8/94	9/01	6/03	Arriva The Shires (3245)
3246	M846 DDS	Volvo B6-50	Alexander	B40F	8/94	8/01		Arriva The Shires (3246)

NOTES

101/2 were renumbered 4305/44, 220, 299, 301/36 were renumbered 5360/9/1/66, 419/20/2/30 were renumbered 3419/20/2/30 in 1/99

101 (BAZ 7384) was previously registered C210 PPE

102 (HDZ 8354) was previously registered C566 LOG, 245 DOC and originally C904 JOF

3335 (H350 PNO) was previously registered H20 BUS, A19 BUS and originally H550 AMT

LAST DAYS BY ARRIVA

Left: 2243: R763DUB Mercedes 810D/Plaxton departs Stansted Airport on 5 April 2003 on the last day of operation of service 133 to Braintree bus station, replaced on re-tender by Stansted Transit.

Right: 2382: R952VPU Mercedes 810D/Plaxton arrives at the East Bergholt terminus during the last week of operation in October 2002; replaced by First Eastern Counties service 93.

TOWARDS THE CENTENARY

Fleet No	Reg No	Chassis	Body	Seating	Date New	Date In	Date Out	Ex:-
4335	J56 GCX	DAF SB220LC550	Ikarus	B48F	7/92	4/01		Arriva East Herts & Essex (4335)
4336	J926 CYL	DAF SB220LC550	Ikarus	B48F	3/92	4/01		Arriva East Herts & Essex (4336)
4337	J927 CYL	DAF SB220LC550	Ikarus	B48F	3/92	3/01		Arriva East Herts & Essex (4337)
4339	K124 TCP	DAF SB220LC550	Ikarus	B48F	8/92	3/01		Arriva East Herts & Essex (4339)
3092	H923 LOX	Dennis Dart	Carlyle	B40F	2/91	10/01	2/02	Arriva East Herts & Essex (3092)
2319	L613 FVX	Mercedes 811D	Dormobile	B31F	9/93	6/01	4/02	Arriva Southend (2319)
2388	P478 DPE	Mercedes 711D	Plaxton	B27F	2/97	7/01	5/03	Arriva Southend (2388)
2391	P481 DPE	Mercedes 711D	Plaxton	B27F	2/97	7/01	5/03	Arriva Southend (2391)
2392	P482 DPE	Mercedes 711D	Plaxton	B27F	2/97	7/01	4/04	Arriva Southend (2392)
DS15	M526 TPM	Dennis Dart	East Lancs	B40F	6/95	3/02		Arriva Guildford & W Surrey (DS15)
DS19	N539 TPF	Dennis Dart	East Lancs	B40F	11/95	4/02	11/02	Arriva Guildford & W Surrey (DS19)
DS20	N540 TPF	Dennis Dart	East Lancs	B40F	11/95	3/02		Arriva Guildford & W Surrey (DS20)
DS21	N541 TPF	Dennis Dart	East Lancs	B40F	11/95	3/02		Arriva Guildford & W Surrey (DS21)
DS23	N543 TPK	Dennis Dart	East Lancs	B40F	2/96	1/02		Arriva Guildford & W Surrey (DS23)
DS24	N544 TPK	Dennis Dart	East Lancs	B40F	2/96	1/02	3/03	Arriva Guildford & W Surrey (DS24)
610	G610 LPH	Volvo B10M-50	East Lancs	H49/39F	9/89	3/02	11/02	Arriva Guildford & W Surrey (610)
613	G613 LPH	Volvo B10M-50	East Lancs	H49/39F	9/89	4/02		Arriva Guildford & W Surrey (613)
614	G614 LPH	Volvo B10M-50	East Lancs	H48/39F	10/89	3/02		Arriva West Sussex (614)
1461	M461 JPA	Mercedes 811D	Plaxton	B31F	2/95	2/02	5/03	Arriva Kent & Sussex (1461)
1462	M462 JPA	Mercedes 811D	Plaxton	B31F	2/95	2/02	5/03	Arriva Kent & Sussex (1462)
5388	B189 BLG	Leyland Olympian ONLXB/1R	ECW	H45/32F	1/85	3/02	6/02	Arriva Southend (5388)
5403	H263 GEV	Leyland Olympian ON2R50G13Z4	Leyland	H47/31F	7/90	3/02	5/03	Arriva Southend (5403)
4352	M52 AWW	Scania K113CRB	Van Hool	C44Ft	7/95	3/02		Arriva Southend (4352)
4353	M53 AWW	Scania K113CRB	Van Hool	C44Ft	7/95	3/02		Arriva Southend (4353)
2115	N919 ETM	Mercedes 709D	Plaxton	DP27F	10/95	6/02	11/02	Arriva Southend (2115)
617	G617 LPH	Volvo B10M-50	East Lancs	H49/39F	10/89	6/02		Arriva West Sussex (617)
2196	J27 UNY	Leyland Tiger TRCTL10/3ARZM	Plaxton	C53F	1/92	6/02		New Enterprise (2196)
3168	J468 OKP	Dennis Dart	Plaxton	B40F	5/92	5/02		Arriva Kent & Sussex (3168)
2372	R942 VPU	Mercedes O810D	Plaxton	B27F	5/98	8/02		Arriva Southend (2372)
5404	H264 GEV	Leyland Olympian ON2R50G13Z4	Leyland	H47/31F	7/90	11/02		Arriva Southend (5404)
3406	P326 HVX	Dennis Dart SLF	Plaxton	B34F	9/96	2/03		Arriva Southend (3406)
DS4	L506 CPJ	Dennis Dart	East Lancs	B40F	5/94	6/03		Arriva Southend (DS4)
DS6	L508 CPJ	Dennis Dart	East Lancs	B40F	5/94	6/03		Arriva Southend (DS6)
201	L201 YCU	Volvo B6-50	Northern Counties	B39F	2/94	7/03		Arriva Kent Thameside(V201)
7615	G615 LPH	Volvo B10M-50	East Lancs	H49/39F	10/89	9/03		Arriva Kent & Sussex (7615)

NOTE

The fleet list is correct at the time of going to press (May 2004) whilst Arriva Southern Counties order for 61 new buses for Medway may result in ousted vehicles transferred to Colchester.

PSV Licence Discs: in use 50 years ago.

Bus 52: KPU516 AEC Regent II/Massey new 4/47. Each bus was issued with a PSV licence disc which was displayed in the driver's cab alongside the road tax disc. Illustrated examples that were still in the holder when the bus was withdrawn. See 52 at work on page 22 (centre).

DEMONSTRATION VEHICLES 1966 - 1992

Fleet No	Reg No	Chassis	Body	Seating	Date New	Date In	Date Out
D1	KTD 551C	Leyland Atlantean PDR1/1	Park Royal	H41/33F	1/65	29/8/66	9/9/66
D2	LYY 827D	AEC Swift	Marshall	B48D	9/66	10/2/67	16/2/67
D3	JTJ 667F	Leyland Panther PSUR1/1	Park Royal	B48D	5/68	17/2/69	19/2/69
D4	MTJ 665G	Leyland Atlantean PDR1/2	Park Royal	H47/32D	10/68	31/3/69	2/4/69
D5	VWD 451H	Metro-Scania BR110MH	MCW	B40D	11/69	17/2/70	28/12/70
D6	ABU 451J	Seddon RU	Seddon	B45D	1/71	7/2/71	13/2/71
D7	NTW 438M	Ford R1014	Plaxton	B43F	4/74	2/12/74	31/12/74
D8	JWC 525N	Ford R1014	Duple	B45F	6/75	27/4/76	11/5/76
D9	XCW 955R	Leyland National 11351A/1R	Leyland	B49F	1/77	6/3/77	19/3/77
D9	XCW 955R	Leyland National 11351A/1R	Leyland	B49F	1/77	28/11/77	11/12/77
D10	NRN 558T	Leyland National 11351A/1R	Leyland	B49F	1/79	28/11/79	12/12/79
D11	WRN 413V	Leyland National 2 NL116L11/11R	Leyland	B49F	1/80	21/8/80	1/9/80
D12	THM 667M	Daimler Fleetline CRL6	MCW	H45/32F	6/74	20/8/82	15/1/83
D13	JGF 321K	Daimler Fleetline CRG6LXB	Park Royal	H44/24D	5/72	2/11/83	9/11/83
D14	A308 RSU	Volvo B10M-50	East Lancs	H47/36F	10/83	4/6/84	20/6/84
D15	A77 FRY	Dennis Dominator	East Lancs	H43/33F	12/83	1/7/84	8/7/84
D16	TBC 51X	Dennis Dominator	East Lancs	H43/33F	10/81	8/7/84	15/7/84
D17	A33 MRN	Leyland Olympian ONTL11/2R	ECW	H47/27F	3/84	20/7/84	6/8/84
D18	A499 NHG	Leyland DAB 9/948L	DAB	B43F	3/84	22/3/86	5/4/86
D19	E566 JFR	Leyland Swift	Wadham Stringer	B37F	11/87	30/12/87	5/1/88
D20	E76 TDA	MCW Metrorider MF150/5	MCW	B25F	10/87	7/1/88	13/1/88
D21	E36 VKP	Iveco 49.10	Dormobile	B25F	12/87	26/1/88	15/2/88
D22	E576 ANE	Renault S56	NCME	B25F	3/88	12/4/88	22/4/88
D23	E425 XKU	Renault S56	Reeve Burgess	B25F	1/88	18/4/88	27/4/88
D24	E365 KKV	Talbot Express	Talbot	B20F	1/88	8/6/88	20/6/88
D25	E456 VUM	Mercedes 811D	Optare	B31F	6/88	27/6/88	4/7/88
D26	E637 TOG	MCW Metrorider MF158/1	MCW	B33F	10/87	19/7/88	21/7/88
D27	G785 PWL	DAF SB220LC550	Optare	B47F	8/89	21/11/89	28/11/89
D28	F682 DWT	DAF SB220LC550	Optare	B47F	4/89	24/11/89	28/11/89
D29	G113 SKX	Scania N113CRB	Alexander	B53F	8/89	22/3/90	27/3/90
D30	G81 VFW	Dennis Dominator	Alexander	H45/33F	2/90	17/4/90	24/6/90
D31	F682 SRN	Leyland Tiger TRCL10/3ZRA	Plaxton	C53F	8/88	3/5/90	10/5/90
D32	F100 AKB	Renault PR100/2	NCME	B51F	10/88	17/7/90	6/8/90
D33	H908 DTP	Dennis Dart	Wadham Stringer	B35F	1/81	4/3/91	10/3/91
D34	J367 BNW	MAN 11.190	Optare	B40F	3/92	8/11/92	13/11/92

The above vehicles were provided by the chassis and/or body manufacturers, except D12 (supplied by Ensignbus, dealers, Purfleet) and D13 (loaned by Brockhouse-Maxwell Transmissions, West Bromwich). D15/D16 were borrowed from Leicester City Transport and D30 was borrowed from Grimsby-Cleethorpes Transport, all three by arrangement with Dennis Bros., Guildford.

NOTE:

The foregoing fleet list is a simplified listing of all the vehicles which have operated from the Magdalen Street depot under the municipal ownership, excluding buses loaned from Great Yarmouth, Hedingham, Ipswich, Maidstone & District, Northumbria, Reading and Southend which retained the owning operators fleetnumbers. Under Arriva ownership, there have been numerous short term loans from other companies within the Group including Arriva The Shires and Arriva Southern Counties, often only staying a few days. If a vehicle has not been shown on the official fleet-list issued locally it has not been included above. Readers seeking full details of these, plus chassis and/or body numbers, and subsequent owners of fleet vehicles, are recommended to the PSV Circle Publication 3PF7 "Colchester Corporation and Successors" published in July 2002.

SIGNIFICANT TESTS

Left: D1: KTD552C The first rear engined/front entranced double decker to work a Colchester CT route, shown in Dugard Avenue after reversing into Oaklands Avenue 31 August 1966. Colchester subsequently ordered 10 Leyland PDR1/1 delivered 1967/8. The bus later entered regular service with Wood, Mirfield, Yorks operating into Dewsbury. Right: D17: A33MRN always intended to join the Preston BT fleet and demonstrated throughout the UK in cream and blue. Seen on 3 August 1984 turning into Queen Street from the bus station. Powered by the Leyland TL11 unit, Colchester BT specified Gardner engines in 4 ECW and Cummins in 5 Leyland built (to ECW design) bodies on similar Olympians.

GR Mills(2)

FORM P.S.V. 4   CERTIFICATE No. **F**   07318

ROAD TRAFFIC ACT, 1930.

CERTIFICATE OF FITNESS.

I, the undersigned, a CERTIFYING OFFICER duly appointed by the Minister of Transport, hereby certify, in accordance with the provisions of the Road Traffic Act, 1930, that the vehicle described below fulfils the prescribed conditions as to fitness in respect of its use as a...*Stage*...... carriage.

DESCRIPTION OF VEHICLE.

Index mark and registration number (See Note below)...*VW 4389*...

Make, model and year of manufacture of chassis...*DENNIS G 1928*...

Chassis Number...*70195*...   Seating Capacity, Lower deck...*18*...

Upper deck...*N/h*...

General description :—

(i) Four wheeled or six wheeled...*Four*...

(ii) Pneumatic tyred or otherwise...*Pneumatic*...

(iii) Single or double decked...*Single*...

(iv) Type of body...*Saloon*...

This Certificate shall continue in force until...*24th February 1942*...

Date of issue...*25 FEB 1939*...

Fee £3

Certifying Officer.

NOTE.

If the vehicle does not appear to have been registered under the Roads Act, 1920, that fact will be indicated. In such case the holder of this certificate is required to notify the index mark and registration number of the vehicle to the Commissioners immediately after it has been assigned and to send or deliver this certificate to them for endorsement accordingly.

Bus 47: Note the precise detail of the livery quoted

Top left: 31: GVW947 AEC Regent/Massey when brand-new in March 1939. One of the first 5 Diesel buses. Note the protective chrome bars.

Top right: 44: JVW582 Guy Arab II/Strachan seen in Churchill Way, Barn Hall Estate during April 1960 on a special farewell tour encompassing many non-bus routes. RN Collins

Centre left: 50: KEV804 Bristol K6A/Park Royal awaiting the crowds at Colchester United's football ground in Layer Road, during April 1962; in company with other Bristol K6A and a Daimler CVD6/Roberts. GR Mills

Centre right: 52: KPU516 AEC Regent II/Massey circumnavigates the Albert roundabout en-route to Colchester's North Station during December 1965. GR Mills

Bottom left: 4: OHK432 Daimler CVD6/Roberts the 'lucky' one of the quintet, being picked out for preservation. Seen in Bishops Stortford bound for Lincoln in October 1968. GR Mills

Bottom right: 10: WPU732 AEC Regent III/Massey about to return to the depot from the bus station in October 1970 after yet another successful farewell tour, to a type. GR Mills

GENERAL MANAGERS IN MUNICIPAL OWNERSHIP 1904-1993

RC Bullough   1904-1925
WH Soulby   1925-1945
RR Macaulay   1945-1946
W Astin   1947-1952
W Kershaw   1952-1953
J Gray   1953-1969
MC Merton   1969-1974
CW Sampson   1974-1993

ACKNOWLEDGEMENTS: Thanks are due to the following contributors:

JE Connor, Connor & Butler Ltd., Colchester (1913 Rail crash detail)
Andrew Coleman, Norwich (typesetting main text)
Bob Franklin (tram crew uniform buttons)
Richard Lewis Publicity Manager, Arriva Southern Counties
Colin Mills (proofreading and all minor corrections to captions and text)
Sarah Mills (typesetting photo captions and early maps)
Keith Sadler (regular updates on Arriva fleet/timetable changes)
Christine Stafford (gold ticket machine loan)
Mrs GW Tierney (inspectors compound in depot photo)
Fred Whittaker (uniform and tram timetable loan)

All photographs have been individually credited where known otherwise they have been provided from the collections of:
R Nicolas Collins, Ralph Eves, Geoff Mills and Roger Tuke all of whom contributed to the ticket selections shown on the inside front covers.

REFERENCES:
Colchester Borough Council Minutes and Annual Reports
Essex County Standard Newspapers
The Omnibus Society Publications
The PSV Circle Publications

BACK COVER ILLUSTRATIONS

Top left: 65: NNO65P on an enthusiasts trip to Ipswich is posed up in Constantine Road (behind Ipswich Town F.C. ground) with 65: DPV65D an AEC Regent V/Neepsend during April 1977. Note destination displays which each mention the neighbouring town.   GR Mills

Top right: 82: YNO82S Colchester's BT's first all-over advert was taken-up by the local newspaper as shown when freshly repainted in April 1979 passing through the bus station. Osbornes, Tollesbury 19: XTG378H Leyland Leopard/Willowbrook can be seen in background.   RN Collins

Centre left: 77: YNO77S makes a chilling sight trudging through the snow during January 1987; at work on service 2A passing East Bay. After twenty years work in Colchester 77 was converted to open top by Guide Friday and worked a Portsmouth tour for three seasons. In 2003 it returned to the borough working a circular tour operated by Phoenix, Maldon in City Sightseeing bright red livery, albeit in more clement weather conditions.   RR Eves

Centre right: 78: YNO78S another bitterly cold scene with snow covered coal heaps in the yard opposite Wivenhoe Rail Station during February 1986 as driver Ernie Rutter waits to return to town. 78 later worked on school contracts with Boons, Boreham until the demise of the latter operations. Early in 2004 the bus was converted to open-top by Talisman, Gt Bromley to work alongside 77 on the City Sightseeing tour of the borough!   RR Eves

Bottom left: 84: MEV84V was repainted into pre-war livery to commemorate 90 years of service. Photographed at Highwoods (Tesco) terminus on 28 July 1994 exactly to the day when the trams had commenced operation in 1904 ninety years earlier. After a very short spell with Beestons, Hadleigh the bus became a special projects mobile exhibition in Cambridgeshire for over five years.   RR Eves

Bottom right: 90: RVW90W on the farewell tour to the faithful thirty makes the fifth of 17 photo-stops on the 35 mile tour of the borough terminii. Seen in Lexden Road, West Bergholt on 5 December 1999. After withdrawal 90 was sold to Boons at Boreham (the fourth of the type owned) but like 77/8 had reached Talisman, Gt Bromley by 2004 but fortunately retained its lid!   GR Mills